BLOODSHED AND THE BIBLE

Laurence J. Naismith

Faithbuilders Publishing UK

Faithbuilders Publishing
12 Dukes Court, Bognor Road,
Chichester, PO19 8FX, United Kingdom
www.faithbuilderspublishing.co.uk

ISBN: 978-1-913181-92-5

British Library Cataloguing in Publication Data. A catalogue record for this book is available from the British Library

Formatted by Faithbuilders Publishing
Cover by Esther Kotecha, EKDesign
Printed in the United Kingdom

CONTENTS

Dedication

Dedicated to the memory of the Reverend Roger Martin and his wife Liz. Roger baptized my wife Maxine and officiated at our wedding.

Their teaching, pastoral care, and friendship is fondly remembered.

Foreword

'Where is God in all of this?'

As a Pastor, I have lost count of the number of times I have been asked this simple, yet almost unanswerable, question. Countless generations of humans, many of them Christian, have struggled to come to terms with how the God that we read of in Jesus, could possibly have allowed, or in some cases commanded, such bloodshed.

As we see the current ruins of Ukraine, as we remember the atrocities of the Holocaust and as we count the cost of our ongoing inhuman treatment of refugees, this question remains unchanged. And largely unanswered.

When asked to write a foreword to this book, I at first felt somewhat daunted. As Laurence's Pastor, fellow theologian, and friend, I would have far preferred him to ask someone more literary and celebrated. However, on reflection, perhaps I am the right choice for I know first-hand something of his rigorous studies in, his complete commitment to, and his love of God's word.

As an eminent Forensic Psychiatrist, Laurence has spent half a lifetime asking (and answering) the questions demanded by the evidence in front of him. His professional background allows him to draw conclusions to these questions with authority and understanding; from an almost unique perspective and from one most qualified to answer.

Laurence shows how in a different time, in a different culture and a different people… the same Jesus and the same God was always present with justice, love, mercy and grace. From the Great Flood, through exiles and on into the New Testament, each chapter enables our understanding of the complexity, the difficulty and horror of some of the incidents of bloodshed in the Bible. This is in part guided and strengthened by patient and concise exegesis, but also enriched by a lifetime of psychological insight and understanding of the 'darker side of life'. With context, cultural understanding and by judicious reference to extra-Biblical literature, we are enabled to see with fresh understanding many of the harsh realities of the Bible narratives that seem so out of step with modern contemporary thinking. Some of the darker character flaws of humanity such as jealousy, revenge and mass murder are dealt with sensitively and with wisdom. Laurence's humour shows through, despite the somewhat un-humorous subject, and his sensitivity is as evident as his desire to enable the reader to draw their own conclusions.

It is this aspect that excites me, for as a regular preacher it is seldom possible to give as much time to exegesis as I would like. Each section is sufficient to prepare a whole sermon series, but it is the addition of a Discussion paragraph at the conclusion of each section that really enables the busy pastor/preacher to benefit from fresh insight and pointers for further investigation.

The questions will not go away anytime soon, but this timely book will go a long way to helping us answer them.

Revd Craig Downes
Senior Minister
Stockton Baptist Church

Chapter One
INTRODUCTION

Causing the death of another human being is an act engendering revulsion in most people. The deliberate and irrevocable termination of someone else's life has for millennia been regarded as a social taboo which has been punished with varying degrees of severity. Right from the third chapter of Genesis where we see the first recorded act of murder, as Cain slays his brother Abel, God's attitude to the taking of human life is readily apparent.

Death is a subject largely avoided in conversation in society today. By the very nature of life itself, there is a continual cycle of births and deaths. While the birth of a baby is generally a happy occasion, and one which is joyfully celebrated, deaths are but little spoken of after the funeral and after the appropriate condolences have been offered to the grieving relatives. This may well reflect to a large extent, the fear and uncertainty with which most of the population probably view the prospect of death, and a desire to avoid such consideration, however inevitable it may be. Thoughts of death and its consequences are thus often repressed, not necessarily on a wholly conscious level.

The almost insatiable desire of the public in general for magazine articles, books, documentaries, and films about well-publicised murder cases would thus seem paradoxical. For reasons that are not wholly clear, it is women who are the most avid followers of true crime stories, including those about serial killers. This rather morbid fascination is undoubtedly, at least in part, because, despite the fearful nature of the subject matter, it is being viewed from a distance. One can see the horror, but from the standpoint of a safe place. In this, the individual is in a similar position to those aficionados of horror movies. The viewer is acting solely in the role of an observer but can still vicariously enjoy the excitement of the events portrayed.

Detective fiction has been enormously popular since the publication of Wilkie Collins' 'Woman in White' in 1859, and much of this has centred around the solving of murder cases. Many of this genre have been made into films and/or television series. I myself have read many of this genre, such as those penned by Agatha Christie, and with enjoyment, although admittedly I have never encountered any murder cases such as she describes!

I spent most of my professional working life as a Consultant Forensic Psychiatrist. Many will not be familiar with this relatively small branch of medicine. Essentially, after qualifying as a doctor, I eventually specialised in psychiatry, and then sub-specialised in the field of forensic psychiatry, which deals with the practice of psychiatry as applied to offenders. I have thus examined and treated a very large number of offenders, both male and female. Amongst that number were many hundreds of murder cases, seen both before and after trial. Alongside my medical qualifications, I also possess degrees in theology. I have brought together both fields in the preparation of this book. Despite the plethora of technical words and phrases in both fields, this book is intended for the average reader, and technical terminology has been kept to a minimum. Where employed, it is explained in relatively straightforward terms.

Although my personal knowledge and involvement with homicide cases on a professional basis has now ceased, and I pay only limited attention to the media reporting of such events and the trial proceedings which follow, I still find it fascinating to look at homicide from a theological standpoint and see how it is treated in the Bible. This book, written over 1500 or so years by multiple authors, encompassing many different countries, peoples, cultures, legal and governmental systems, contains much of interest in terms of its portrayal of the causation of death by one individual on another. More importantly, the Bible gives us the definitive word on homicide: that of God.

Some readers will probably have picked up this book, having been attracted by the nature of the subject content. Nevertheless, for Christian readers, it is hoped that they also wish to be aware of theological aspects of the causation of death and related issues. As is clear, the elements involved are not merely restricted to the subject of murder as we commonly regard it but can be seen to include issues of immense significance and importance in today's world, such as abortion, assisted dying (euthanasia), the death penalty, and genocide. All these areas involve the termination of human life in one way or another. Abortion, these days, is carried out as a matter of routine, and its implications attract but little serious attention. Admittedly, there are protesters who are often vocal in their opposition, and these usually have a religious basis for their viewpoint. Nevertheless, the impression is that the world largely views them as a nuisance, rather than taking their expressed concerns in a serious manner.

Euthanasia is the deliberate ending of life before it would occur through natural means. The death penalty involves the judicial termination of life following conviction for an offence or offences for which this is the prescribed penalty. Genocide involves the deliberate killing of a large number of people, usually of a particular ethnic group. What all the aforementioned have in common is that they involve the deliberate killing of human beings by other human beings. Thus, although homicide in legal terms (in the UK) is restricted to the offences of murder, manslaughter, infanticide, and causing death by dangerous driving, one can readily appreciate that other acts are morally, if not legally, closely associated. Nonetheless, this volume will largely restrict its ambit to consideration of the killing of humankind after parturition (birth), and not consider euthanasia or the death penalty. Particularly as this is written largely for a Christian readership, the book will also include events where death has been effected from a divine source.

Christians often have views on these subjects, but all too often these are not well thought out and are formed with minimal recourse to Scripture. I would argue that Christians *should* have an informed opinion on all these issues, and further, that they should be able to express their views in at least a rudimentary form. To be able to do so, they should be aware of the issues involved and, importantly, what Scripture has to say about them. Such is the main focus of this book.

It should also be borne in mind that the Old Testament is a very honest book, even about the failures and sins of its main characters, and just because the stories are told, this does not imply God's approval of everything (as is the case in several stories from Judges). The reader might find all the stories of killing in this book somewhat depressing but remember that God does not take pleasure in the death of a human being but rather urges them to repent and serve him! As it states in Ezekiel 18:30-32:

> Therefore, you Israelites, I will judge each of you according to your own ways, declares the Sovereign Lord. Repent! Turn away from all your offences; then sin will not be your downfall. Rid yourselves of all the offences you have committed, and get a new heart and a new spirit. Why will you die, people of Israel? For I take no pleasure in the death of anyone, declares the Sovereign Lord. Repent and live!

This book is not just about the justice of God, it is also about his grace and love.

Life

Christians believe the biblical account in Genesis when it informs that God created all things. Notably we read in relation to the creation of humankind that, 'God created mankind in his own image, in the image of God he created them; male and female he created them'. (Genesis 1:27)

Acres of print have been devoted to the subject of humans as the image of God, and they will not be rehearsed here. Berkhof,[1] and Letham[2] provide helpful descriptions of the major denominational positions on the matter. For simplicity we will utilise Ross'[3] interpretation:

---

[1] L. Berkhof, *Systematic Theology* (Grand Rapids, Eerdmans, 1941), p.205-208.

[2] Robert Letham, *Systematic Theology* (Wheaton: Crossway, 2019), p.328-334.

[3] Allan Ross, in *Genesis, Exodus*, Cornerstone (Carol Stream: Tyndale House, 2008), p.39-40.

> Only human life is called God's image. The term "image" applies equally to male and female, for that is what makes up the human race. It is used figuratively here, and does not refer to physical shape or outer appearance. Being the image of God means that humans share, although imperfectly, in the nature of God – that is, they were given the communicable attributes of intelligence, knowledge, spiritual understanding, creativity, wisdom, love, compassion, holiness, justice and the like. As the text will explain (2:7)[4], all these capacities were given by the inbreathing of the breath of life. Thus, humans have the capacity to commune with the living God, as well as with one another.

Essentially, God has created all things, but human beings are the one part of his creation who are made in the image of God, and who can communicate with God. This makes man unique in all of creation. There is a degree of affinity between God and man which does not exist in respect of the whole of the rest of creation. This is still the case after the fall, and the entry of sin into the world. Thus, to take a human life, as Grudem puts it, 'is to attack the part of creation that most resembles God, and it betrays an attempt or desire (if one were able) to attack God himself.'[5]

When described in these terms, some appreciation of the awful gravity of the offence can be appreciated. This only deepens on reflection, when one can begin to recognise the implications of the taking of human life. It would be well to bear this in mind through the reading of the rest of this book.

Homicide

It is essential that there is an initial understanding of what is meant by the word 'homicide'. Many will think it refers merely to murder (and perhaps manslaughter). Care needs to be taken here as the criminal law varies in different countries, but in the UK the word 'homicide' encompasses the following offences:

---

[4] Genesis 2:7

[5] Wayne Grudem, *Systematic Theology* (Leicester: IVP, 1994), p.444.

(1) Murder
(2) Manslaughter
(3) Infanticide
(4) Causing death by dangerous driving

Abortion (the deliberate termination of a human pregnancy), and euthanasia (the painless killing of a patient suffering from an incurable and painless disease or in an irreversible coma) can be considered as matters related to the concept of homicide.

One important point to make from the outset is that the legal statutes of a particular country in a particular age cannot be regarded as a reliable indicator of compliance with what is directed by Scripture, or what can be reasonably inferred from the pages of the Bible. It is often in these circumstances that Christians struggle to make decisions as to what is right, and at this point it is appropriate to briefly consider the discipline of apologetics.

Apologetics

The word 'apologetics' is frequently misunderstood in Christian circles. This is likely due to its similarity to the word 'apology', and its meaning in the vernacular. Apologetics is *not* about apologising for being a Christian or having Christian faith!

The Greek word *apologia* means 'to give an answer', and it is from this that we get the word 'apologetics', which is used to describe the intellectual defence of the Christian faith from outside attacks and criticisms. The Apostle Peter enjoins us as follows, 'Always be prepared to give an answer to everyone who asks you to give the reason for the hope that you have'. (1 Peter 3:15)

The above verse is sometimes referred to as the *locus classicus* for apologetics, by which is meant it is the classical Scriptural location to support the discipline of apologetics. R. C. Sproul[6] points out that Peter's admonition, 'be ready', is reminiscent of the Boy Scout's motto, 'Be prepared'. All Christians need to be able to defend their faith and the beliefs which are inherent in that faith. This is the responsibility of the individual Christian and not one which can be

[6] R. C. Sproul, *1-2 Peter* (Sanford: Reformation Trust, 2019), p.97.

passed on to a minister or others in the church. Of necessity, this implies that each Christian should have some familiarity with the Bible and its teachings. They should have a grounding in basic doctrinal principles.

It is not being suggested that all Christians should be apologists in the formal sense of the word. One can think of well-known figures who are or have been are prominent in this field, such as Norman Geisler, Alistair McGrath, and James White and, clearly, the average Christian cannot hope to emulate prominent individuals such as these in logical thought and breadth of knowledge. Neither are they expected to do so. Nevertheless, although all Christians, by definition, have faith, this is not blind faith. They are trusting in Christ for salvation with all that that entails. They should be able to communicate the basic truths of the gospel to others and to defend their beliefs in these circumstances.

When it comes to Christian ethics, as has already been noted, not all believers necessarily sing from the same hymn sheet, as it were. Some will not enter a shop on a Sunday, whereas others will happily go to the supermarket after church. Whereas core doctrinal teachings, such as the concept of the Trinity, are non-negotiable, secondary issues (sometimes referred to by the Greek term *adiaphora*), are not universally accepted and agreed, and can lead to disagreement and even argument amongst committed Christians.

In such circumstances, Christians, through prayer and the reading of Scripture, have to come to their own conclusions in clear conscience. Such a process has much in common with the process involved in apologetics. One is coming to one's conclusions on the basis of rational argument based on the evidence, but in this instance the argument/discussion is not with other individuals, but one is debating with one's own self; weighing the pros and cons of particular factors in order to reach a decision. Obviously here the reading of non-Scriptural materials and discussion with others will also influence those conclusions reached.

In this book, an attempt will be made to enhance individual knowledge of the basic biblical principles pertaining to the matters at hand. It is nevertheless accepted that while core doctrinal principles such as the Trinity, and salvation through faith alone in

Christ alone, are not negotiable, there have always been some issues, for example, paedobaptism (the baptism of infants), and eschatology (the theology of end times), where genuine Christians can disagree. And so it is here. For example, no Christian is likely to argue that premeditated murder is not wrong, but while some will undoubtedly support the death penalty, others do not.

It is not the purpose of this author to assert particular viewpoints where the Scriptural position is not crystal clear. Admittedly, the author's personal preferences may inadvertently be apparent, but I have striven to present the relevant arguments in such cases, in order to leave the reader to come to their own conclusions. This is not intended as a book where the purpose is merely to educate – here, the reader is expected to weigh the arguments and draw their own conclusions, and that in such a way as to be able to justify their conclusions both to themselves and to others.

The law

It is important to remember that although Christians are subject to the law of whatever land they live in, that they are ultimately responsible to a higher power, that of God. They are to be subject to their government (Romans 13:1-3; Titus 3:1; 1 Peter 2:13), although not when this is in conflict with God's law (Acts 5:29). Thus, whereas abortion is legal in the UK under defined parameters, this in itself does not automatically imply that it is a right and proper option or recourse for the Christian.

We also need to bear in mind that Jesus' teaching in the Sermon on the Mount (Matthew 5-7) in the case of murder, amplifies and extends the Mosaic law. Specifically, in relation to the sixth commandment ('You shall not murder', Exodus 20:13), he points to the underlying cognitive state which presages murder and indicates that this too is meritorious of judgement, that is, it too is sinful. As MacArthur[7] notes:

> In saying, **But I say to you**, Jesus was not contrasting His teaching with that of the Old Testament (cf. Matthew. 5:17-19) but with that of rabbinic tradition. He

[7] John MacArthur, *Matthew 1-7* (Chicago, Moody, 1985), p.292.

> was saying, in effect, 'Let me tell what the Scriptures themselves say, what God's truth is on the matter. You cannot justify yourselves because you have not committed the physical act of murder. Murder goes much deeper than that. It originates in the heart, not in the hands. It starts with evil thoughts, regardless of whether or not those thoughts are brought to consummation in action.'

A similar, but more forceful point is made in 1 John. 3:15: 'Anyone who hates a brother or sister is a murderer'. Although the issue will not be laboured here, Jesus is making the point, obvious to all, that the act of intentionally causing the death of another, is not one which suddenly arises *de novo*. There are precursors in the emotions, and these themselves are sinful in nature. Jesus points not just to the physical act of effecting the death of another, but to the antecedent sinful lines of thinking in the heart. The Sadducees and Pharisees of Jesus' time were concentrating on the letter of the Mosaic law in this (and other) areas, and this blinded them to the sinful thoughts which underpinned the act of murder. Jesus was concerned with the underlying implications of the divine commands. He was concerned with the principles on which the law was based. This was an approach in stark contrast to that of the Pharisees. Where there was no biblical law for, for example, the distance one could travel on the Sabbath, they invented one and regarded this man-made rule as authoritative, treating it as if it had the authority of Scripture. Nevertheless, this did not preclude them from inventing ways of circumventing their own created rules! Jesus was giving the Pharisees a lesson in biblical exegesis. He was teaching the teachers how to interpret Scripture!

I would make this point forcefully because when, later in this book, we look at motives for murder, we come back to this point. Readers might find it useful to consider the thoughts which preceded actual physical murder, and their own thought life. You might conclude that murderous thoughts and potential actions are not quite as far away from your own position as you might previously have felt assured!

Organisational approach

So far as classification is concerned, there are obvious difficulties. Were we approaching this on the basis of crime figures today, we would doubtless be much more informed about such details as age of the perpetrator and the age of the victim. We would have other pertinent details such as their sex, age, marital status, occupation, and many others. We could then classify them in a variety of ways. However, the Bible is a theological document and not designed to give us information which, although it would doubtless be interesting and satisfy our intellectual curiosity, is not essential to its core purpose. The relevant section headings are therefore not satisfactory to the logical mind. Although one may be able to identify what appears to be the principal motive, one cannot assume a single motive, and often several different factors are in operation. Matters are not always as clear cut as one might like to think. Additionally, although there are recognisable patterns in killing, one cannot assume that those deaths recorded in the Bible are a representative picture of killings in biblical times in terms of perpetrators, victims, or motives.

Final introductory comment

It should be noted that the events referred to and described in this book do not encompass all the circumstances resulting in unnatural death in the pages of Scripture. They do, however, provide a fair representation, and a basis for the consideration of others.

Lastly, it is important to remember that the Bible should not be read as if it was yesterday's newspaper. We are (understandably) prone to think of events in the Bible as if they occurred in our own time and culture. To do so constitutes serious error. When the episodes described here occurred, they did so in times and cultures far removed from our own. Admittedly, human emotions have not changed in the intervening years, although their mode of expression is heavily influenced by their cultural substrate. Legal frameworks were much less sophisticated and talk of human rights and international conventions virtually non-existent. Read of these events (and indeed the rest of Scripture) with this in mind.

Chapter Two

THE LAW

Those offences which comprise homicide in UK law have already been identified in the introductory chapter. Murder and manslaughter are obvious sub-categories and causing death by dangerous driving does not apply to biblical considerations. Essentially, we are looking at the offences of murder and manslaughter.

Although most, if not all, countries have legislation which encompasses these two categories, the law varies from jurisdiction to jurisdiction and in terms of its historical development. This is a complex area, but for the purposes of this consideration it is not necessary to explore the legal provision in undue detail. Given that the cases to be examined are taken from both Old and New Testament periods and that we are looking to make a comparison with the situation today, it is necessary to first examine the Old Testament law, essentially that which is contained in the Pentateuch, the first five books of the Bible.

Additionally, the law in first century Palestine must be considered. Here, amongst the Jewish population, Old Testament stipulations still applied so far as they were concerned. Nevertheless, with the expansion of the Roman Empire and the occupation of Jerusalem by Pompey in 63 BC, the Romans controlled Palestine (as well as adjoining Syria and Egypt) and the occupying power had supreme authority over the legal process. For the purpose of comparison, a summary of current UK law in this area will be provided.

Old Testament Law on Homicide

Murder

Foremost here is the offence of murder. At the outset it is essential to place this crime in its theological setting. First it is necessary to turn to Genesis 9:5-7:

And for your lifeblood I will surely demand an accounting. I will demand an accounting from every animal. And from each human being too, I will demand an accounting for the life of another human being.

> Whoever sheds human blood, by humans shall their blood be shed; for in the image of God has God made mankind.
>
> As for you, be fruitful and increase in number; multiply on the earth and increase upon it.

Man was created in the image of God (Genesis 1:26-27) and thus, murder can be properly viewed as sacrilege (a violation of what is regarded as sacred). As Mathews[8] points out, 'to take human life unlawfully therefore is to usurp God's sovereignty over life and death.'

The prohibition against murder is made explicit in the decalogue (the Ten Commandments). In Exodus 20:13 the sixth commandment instructs, 'You shall not murder' and this precept is reiterated in Deuteronomy 5:17.

It is worth noting here that the King James version of the Bible, which still has many adherents today, uses the word 'kill' rather than 'murder'. This has led to unfortunate misunderstandings as to the precise nature of the offence which is proscribed here. In a partial defence of the use of the term 'kill', Stuart[9] notes that in the seventeenth century, this word included the sense of murder more often than it does today.

---

[8] Kenneth A. Mathews, *Genesis 1-11:26*, NAC (Nashville: B&H, 1966), p.405.
[9] Douglas K. Stuart, *Exodus*, NAC (Nashville: B&H, 2006), p.462.

There is a single penalty for murder: death. Leviticus 24:17 states that 'Anyone who takes the life of a human being is to be put to death'. The same point is also made in Exodus 21:12, 14, 20; Numbers 35:16-21, 30, and Deuteronomy 19:11-13.

Manslaughter

As does modern law, the Old Testament distinguishes between deliberate and accidental killing, the difference between the premeditated act of effecting the death of another, and its accidental causation. Simply put, to deliberately kill another human being constitutes murder, while killing another human being without intending to do so is manslaughter. In current UK law the penalty for murder is life imprisonment, and while this sentence can also be passed in cases of manslaughter, so can lesser sentences, even probation.

In Numbers 35 we find a clear distinction between the act of murder and its penalty (verses 16-21), and the accidental killing of another. This is documented as follows in verses 22-23:

> But if without enmity someone suddenly pushes another or throws something at them unintentionally or, without seeing them, drops on them a stone heavy enough to kill them, and they die, then since that other person was not an enemy and no harm was intended, the assembly must judge between the accused and the avenger of blood according to these regulations.

The perpetrator of the accidental homicide would flee from the revenge of the bereaved family to one of the assigned cities of refuge. A trial would then take place, probably by a group of citizens. If the accused was not found guilty of murder, he could remain in the city of refuge until the death of the high priest. The significance of the latter point is not wholly clear. The death of the high priest may have been considered a substitute for the manslayer himself, or it may have marked the end of a mandatory period (akin to a prison sentence) separated from conventional life.

Roman law on homicide

Unsurprisingly, over the course of around 1,000 years, first in the Republic, and then in the Empire, Roman law changed. The time of particular interest of this book is that of the first century AD, when the events of the New Testament occurred, and the books themselves were written.

It is difficult to comment briefly on the Roman law and court system as it was so different from that of today, despite its influence on the modern legal system. Some preliminary remarks can be helpfully made. First, justice was not uniformly applied, as we expect today. Penalties for the higher social classes, such as those from the senatorial and equestrian classes, tended to be less severe than for the lower ranks of society. It almost goes without saying that slaves were dealt with more harshly. Second, the concept of prison was very different from how we view it today. There was no concept of custodial sentences as a punishment. Prisons were places where the accused were held pre-trial, and the convicted until execution (these tended be brief periods). Third, although there were both civil and criminal courts in Rome, they were rather different from those today. Many criminal offences today were tried in the civil courts in Rome. Indeed, most crimes of violence were tried in Roman civil courts.

Homicide within the family circle appears to have accounted for most of the murders in Roman times, and indeed, this is broadly the case today, if one uses the concept of the extended family. These fell within the jurisdiction of the *paterfamilias*, who was the male head of the household, and had absolute authority over it. For example, when a child was born, it was his decision whether the child was permitted to live or die.

So far as murder is concerned, the intention to kill was necessary (just as it is today). Killing in self-defence was justifiable homicide. The penalty for murder was death in most cases, although those of higher social status would be more likely to have all their property seized and be exiled.

Current law on homicide

Here, we are predominately concerned with UK law.

Murder can be considered as unlawful homicide committed with 'malice aforethought'. In simple terms, the perpetrator must have committed the unlawful act with what can be referred to as a 'guilty mind'. They must have had what might be termed 'evil intent'. Matters are not quite as clearly cut as this might suggest, but in simple terms this is adequate for our purposes here.

There is only one penalty upon conviction for murder in the UK courts, and that is life imprisonment. The judge will impose a minimum tariff – the minimum length of imprisonment the prisoner must serve prior to release. It should be noted that this does not in itself imply that the inmate will be released after serving that length of time. That will come under the province of the Parole Board. Very occasionally, where the features of the offence are particularly atrocious, a whole life sentence might be imposed. This means that the convicted individual must potentially spend the rest of their life in prison. There are only a handful of such cases in the English penal system, and I can only recall seeing one in the UK, although I have come across others in North American correctional facilities.

Manslaughter covers several types of unlawful homicide which do not constitute murder. It can be subdivided into voluntary manslaughter and involuntary manslaughter.

Essentially, the issue of voluntary manslaughter arises when, despite the presence of the criteria for murder being fulfilled (in simple terms, having committed the guilty act and having the guilty mind – the evil intention), there is a partial defence, sufficient to reduce the defendant's liability to voluntary manslaughter. These are loss of self-control, diminished responsibility, and a suicide pact. It is not necessary to pursue these in detail, but as it is frequently used as a defence in murder cases, and reported in the media, it is appropriate to make some reference to the concept of diminished responsibility.

When diminished responsibility is successfully argued by the defence on behalf of a client facing a murder charge, the verdict is one of manslaughter rather than murder. This 'unties' the hands of the sentencing judge who otherwise (on a conviction for murder) would have no option other than to impose a life sentence. Without going into detail, the accused must have had an abnormality of mental functioning arising from a recognised medical condition which substantially impaired their mental ability to understand the nature of their conduct and/or form a rational judgement and/or exercise self-control. The decision as to whether the defence of diminished responsibility is successful or not is one for the jury.

It is in relation to the issue of diminished responsibility where forensic psychiatrists become involved. This is not at all a straightforward area, and it is not rare for there to be disagreement between psychiatric experts for the defence and the prosecution. I can attest that giving evidence in such circumstances can be a stressful business indeed!

Genocide

Given the divinely sanctioned violence toward other peoples during the Israelite advance into the promised land, it is appropriate to consider the law relating to genocide.

Genocide is different from the criminal laws of the country in which we live because it is a distinct form of criminal legislation that crosses international boundaries. It was first recognised as a crime by the United Nations General Assembly in 1948. Article II reads as follows:

> In the present Convention, genocide means any of the following acts committed with intent to destroy, in whole or part, a national, ethical, racial or religious group as such:
>
> a. Killing members of the group;
> b. Causing serious bodily or mental harm to members of the group;
> c. Deliberately inflicting on the group conditions of life calculated to bring about its physical destruction in whole or in part;
> d. Imposing measures intended to prevent births within the group;
> e. Forcibly transferring children of the group to another group.

Although genocide was not officially regarded as a crime before 1948, it is obvious that events fulfilling the 1948 criteria have taken place with alarming regularity throughout human history. For example, even in relatively modern times, the Political Instability Task Force (a U.S. government sponsored research project), estimated that around 50 million deaths had occurred between 1956 and 2016 in 43 separate occurrences of genocide.

It is readily apparent that our current laws on homicide owe much to those principles outlined in the Old Testament law. Our legal system also owes much to the Roman legal system, although this is less obvious from the information presented here. One intended function of this book is to facilitate comparison between the cases in this book, particularly from the Old Testament, and the legislation of today.

Chapter Three

GOD EFFECTS DEATH

Introduction

The term 'act of God' is sometimes used to refer to a natural untoward event outside of human control, such as a tsunami or an earthquake. Although it is not uncommon to hear the expression in everyday conversation, its legal use largely relates to contracts, often for insurance purposes, where acts of God provisions, often referred to as 'Force Majeure' clauses, relate to events outside human control, such as the two mentioned above. Our concerns here, however, are not related to the world of insurance contracts.

As Christians we recognise that God is sovereign, and recognise with Macleod[10] that this includes at least three things:

1. *Ownership.* Everything belongs to God
2. *Authority.* God has an absolute right to impose his will
3. *Control.* God is master of his universe

Psalm 135:6 tells us 'The Lord does whatever pleases him, in the heavens and on the earth, in the seas and all their depths'. King Nebuchadnezzar, on recovering his sanity, praised God and said:

> His dominion is an eternal dominion; his kingdom endures from generation to generation. All the peoples of the earth are regarded as nothing. He does as he pleases with the powers of heaven and the peoples of the

---

[10] D. Macleod, in *New Dictionary of Theology* (Downers Grove: IVP, 1988), p.654-656.

> earth. No one can hold back his hand or say to him: 'What have you done?' (Daniel 4:34-35)

In addition to the sovereignty of God, it is also necessary to have an appreciation of the holiness of God. It is one of the essential divine attributes and is one of absolute moral perfection. There is a clear consequence from this for the human race. God abhors sin and demands his judgement on sin. Nevertheless, God in his grace and mercy sent his Son to die at Calvary that our sins could be imputed to him, and his righteousness imputed to us at conversion. Those not so justified face eternity in hell.

Although God's final judgement will be faced by all, and the sheep separated from the goats, God has the right to bring judgement at any time. Indeed, it is only his patient forbearing that means sinful people continue to exist at all. God owes the human race nothing other than his judgement. This vital truth should be borne in mind, not only here, but also in the following chapter relating to the deaths of those in ethnic groupings distinct from the Israelites. Too many people labour under the misapprehension that God owes us something, or that we deserve something from God. He doesn't, and we don't.

We are all aware that there will be a final judgement (Psalm 96:13), but too often, we ignore judgement in the present life. As Morris[11] points out:

> God's present judgement of people is forcefully brought out in Romans 1 with its threefold "God gave them over" (vv. 24, 26, 28). God is hostile to every evil and this is made manifest in his judgements here and now.

We should not, and indeed cannot, assume that God's justice and judgement is necessarily deferred in its entirety to the final judgement. In the examples of this chapter, we can readily appreciate that it is not.

---

[11] Leon Morris, in *Evangelical Dictionary of Biblical Theology*, ed. Walter A. Elwell (Grand Rapids: Baker, 1996), p.437.

The Flood

Genesis 6:5-8

> The Lord saw how great the wickedness of the human race had become on the earth, and that every inclination of the thoughts of the human heart was only evil all the time. The Lord regretted that he had made human beings on the earth, and his heart was deeply troubled. So the Lord said, 'I will wipe from the face of the earth the human race I have created – and with them the animals, the birds and the creatures that move along the ground – for I regret that I have made them.' But Noah found favour in the eyes of the Lord.

Genesis 7:17-23

> For forty days the flood kept coming on the earth, and as the waters increased they lifted the ark high above the earth. The waters rose and increased greatly on the earth, and the ark floated on the surface of the water. They rose greatly on the earth, and all the high mountains under the entire heavens were covered. The waters rose and covered the mountains to a depth of more than fifteen cubits. Every living thing that moved on land perished – birds, livestock, wild animals, all the creatures that swarm over the earth, and all mankind. Everything on dry land that had the breath of life in its nostrils died. Every living thing on the face of the earth was wiped out; people and animals and the creatures that move along the ground and the birds were wiped from the earth. Only Noah was left, and those with him in the ark.

The story of the flood is not limited to the Bible but exists in the cultural heritage of other civilisations as well. Probably the best known is the Epic of Gilgamesh, a poem from ancient Mesopotamia. Although this will not be examined here in any detail, two things are worthy of mention. First, it asserts that the people on earth were making too much noise and that is why the gods were annoyed. Second, the gods discussed among themselves the justification for a destructive universal flood.[12] Although this account does have some similarity to the biblical account of the flood in that there was divine disapproval of the human race, and in the concept of an overwhelming flood, there are very significant differences as well. For example, in the Gilgamesh story the instrument of deliverance is cuboid in shape as opposed to the boat-like construction of the ark. It does not take much imagination to compare the relative likeliness of seaworthiness of the two configurations. Nevertheless, it is interesting, and reassuring that the flood story is not restricted to biblical sources alone.

As can be readily appreciated from the first passage quoted above, God was aware of the depravity of the humankind he had created and whose nature had become contaminated as the result of Adam's sin. God determined to cleanse the land with a great flood and so destroy the human race.

The passage also indicates that God 'regretted he had made human beings'. This is difficult to understand as God's reasoning is always perfect, and he does not change his mind (Numbers 23:19; 1 Samuel 15:29; Psalm 110:4). This is not an issue which can be explored in detail here, although Walton[13], in the course of offering three possible solutions states, 'We can justify the terminology by seeking to understand ways in which anthropomorphic language is used in describing God's actions without imputing human limitations to him. This is the path followed in most commentaries. By the word 'anthropomorphic' is meant the attribution of human characteristics to the divine nature. Such is not meant to suggest any limitation on the character of God but is a way of describing matters in a way which human beings can understand. Although God is infinite in his attributes, we are not, and this is a method of description which our limited appreciation can comprehend.

Nevertheless, 'Noah found favour in the eyes of the Lord' (Genesis 6:8). In Genesis 6:9, Noah is described as 'a righteous man, blameless among the people of his time, and he walked faithfully

---

[12] Kenneth A. Mathews, *Genesis 1-22:26*, NAC (Nashville: B & H, 1996), p.339.

[13] John H. Walton, *Genesis*, NIVAC (Grand Rapids: Zondervan, 2001), p.308-309.

with God'. This is a remarkable character reference for an individual who had lived for some 600 years in the environment of an exceedingly wicked world. The fact that he is characterised as righteous and blameless is at first glance rather confusing. Paul tells us in Romans 3:10 that 'There is no one righteous, not even one', and similar sentiments are expressed in Psalms 14:1-3, 53:1-3, and Ecclesiastes 7:20. Walton[14] is again of assistance here when he writes:

> His righteousness and blamelessness is *in comparison to the people of his time*. This is in accord with the normal usage of these terms throughout the Old Testament, where they do not generally indicate someone's absolute righteousness or blamelessness relative to God's standards but indicate one's status on the human scale.

The word 'remnant' is found in many places in the Bible. A remnant is something left over, something remaining after others or other things have gone. In the Bible it often refers to the people of God who remain after divine judgement has removed the rest of a population, as can be seen in Ezra 9:15, Micah 2:12, and Romans 9:27. Here, Noah is the faithful remnant in a world characterised by wickedness. God is going to save Noah and his family, even in the midst of destruction.

God tells Noah of his plan to destroy humanity and instructs him to build an ark, provision it, and populate it with animals and Noah's family prior to the deluge. Noah is obedient, constructs the vessel, and enters it at God's command. And so we come to the second passage of Scripture reproduced at the beginning of this section. Noah and his family are secure in the ark despite the flood which has wiped out the rest of humankind. Presently the waters will abate, and he will be able to exit the ark and offer pleasing sacrifices to God.

Tremper Longman III[15] notes that 'All the stories of Genesis 3-11 have a particular structure where a story of sin is followed by a divine judgement speech and ends with the description of the execution of

---

[14] Ibid, p.311.

[15] Tremper Longman III, *Genesis*, SGBC (Grand Rapids: Zondervan, 2016), p.296.

the judgement'. As Romans 6:23 points out, 'the wages of sin is death'. We read this of the character of God in Exodus 34:6, where it states: 'The Lord, the Lord, the compassionate and gracious God, slow to anger, abounding in love and faithfulness', and we also read that he is slow to anger in Numbers 14:18, but despite this forbearance, his patience is not inexhaustible. God is a just God and cannot tolerate sin. Sin is followed by judgement, and here the judgement of God on a sinful world resulted in the obliteration of the human race with the exception of Noah and his family. Was this just? Yes.

The story of the flood can be viewed as a type of the final judgement. In typology, certain people or places in the Old Testament have parallels with people or places in the New Testament and are described as types of these people and places. For example, the animal sacrifices, killed in relation to the atonement for sins in the Old Testament, can be viewed as types of Christ, who was the perfect sacrifice for sin in the New Testament.

It is not difficult to make parallels here. The comparison between the flood and the final judgement is obvious, as is the destruction of most of the earth's population and the survival of a faithful remnant. We are reminded of this in Matthew 24:38-39, Luke 17:27, and 2 Peter 2:5 and 3:5-6. As Walton[16] points out,

> Just as the destruction of the Flood initiated a new beginning for those spared, so Peter indicates that the final judgement will do the same: 'But in keeping with his promise we are looking forward to a new heaven and a new earth, the home of righteousness' (2 Peter 3:13).

NADAB AND ABIHU

Leviticus 10:1-11

> Aaron's sons Nadab and Abihu took their censers, put fire in then and added incense; and they offered unauthorised fire before the Lord, contrary to his command. So fire came out from the presence of the

---

[16] Ibid, p.333.

> Lord and consumed them, and they died before the Lord. Moses then said to Aaron, 'This is what the Lord spoke of when he said: '"Among those who approach me I will be proved holy; In the sight of all the people I will be honoured." '
>
> Aaron remained silent.
>
> Moses summoned Mishael and Elzaphan, sons of Aaron's uncle Uzziel, and said to them, 'Come here; carry your cousins outside the camp, away from the front of the sanctuary.' So they came and carried them, still in their tunics, outside the camp, as Moses ordered.
>
> Then Moses said to his sons Eleazer and Ithamar, 'Do not let your hair become unkempt and do not tear your clothes or you will die and the Lord will be angry with the whole community. But your relatives, all the Israelites, may mourn for those the Lord has destroyed by fire. Do not leave the entrance to the tent of meeting or you will die, because the Lord's anointing oil is on you.' So they did as Moses said.
>
> Then the Lord said to Aaron, 'You and your sons are not to drink wine or other fermented drink whenever you go into the tent of meeting, or you will die. This is a lasting ordinance for the generations to come, so that you can distinguish between the holy and the common, between the unclean and the clean, and so you can teach the Israelites all the decrees the Lord has given them through Moses.'

The events of this chapter stand in contrast to the rest of Leviticus which largely concerns itself with ceremonies and rites. Here, we have a narrative account of events which are admittedly not easy to fully understand in their detail.

Essentially, the first few chapters relate to regulations for sacrificial offerings, burnt offerings, grain offerings, sin offerings etcetera. From chapter eight until the end of chapter ten, there are directions relating to the ordination and service of priests. Chapters 11-15 relate to laws about what is clean and what is unclean. The placement of the story about Nadab and Abihu may thus be regarded as significant in that the regulations for cleanness/uncleanness are preceded by their failure to obey the instructions of God.

Essentially, as the Scripture above notes, Nadab and Abihu 'offered unauthorised fire before the Lord, and they were consumed by heavenly fire'. They died on the spot. It is not exactly clear how they transgressed, although this has been the subject of endless speculation through the centuries. The adjective used to qualify the fire is 'unauthorised' in the NIV, ESV, and CSB translations. The NASB and the KJV have 'strange'. The NLT opts for 'the wrong kind of fire'.

Nadab and Abihu were the two oldest sons of Aaron, who was consecrated as priest, as were his sons, in Leviticus 8-9 (cf. Exodus 28-29). The priesthood was thus assigned to one particular family. As to its function, we are reminded that:

> The Aaronic priesthood was instituted in order to maintain fellowship between the holy God and the sinful nation, to bring the people's gifts and sacrifices before God and to convey God's gifts, mercy, salvation and blessing to the people.[17]

Whatever the reason, something was grossly amiss with the fire to incur God's judgement with divine fire and ensuing calamitous results. Harrison[18] discusses this issue in a helpful manner. Nadab and Abihu would have commenced their duties by taking flat pans (the censers) and putting burning coals in them. Then the incense would have been placed on the coals, and this presented to God. First, there is no indication that the coals had been removed from the altar of burnt offering, the contents of which had been lighted by divine fire when God had sanctified the tabernacle at the priests' consecration. Potentially here, therefore, something not consecrated to the service of God (that is, something unholy) had contaminated the consecrated elements. Second, their act of presenting the incense

---

[17] *The New Unger's Bible Dictionary*, ed. R. K. Harrison (Chicago: Moody, 1988), p.1033.

[18] R. K. Harrison, *Leviticus,* (TOTC), (Downers Grove: IVP, 1980), p. 109-110.

upon coals to God is not contained in the sacrificial regulations for anyone other than the high priest himself. Nadab and Abihu appear to have usurped the duties of the high priest, and despite several possible motivations for so acting, they were not coming from a place of trying to live a life of holiness before God. Essentially, as Harrison suggests, they violate a number of the elements of sacrifice that had been divinely prescribed.

Verses 8-11 state:

> Then the Lord said to Aaron, 'You and your sons are not to drink wine or other fermented drink whenever you go into the tent of meeting, or you will die. This is a lasting ordinance for the generations to come, so that you can distinguish between the holy and the common, between the unclean and the clean, and so you can teach the Israelites all the decrees the Lord has given them through Moses.'

The above has led to the suggestion that their primary offence was appearing before God whilst intoxicated.

Although the Levitical priests had a variety of functions, they might primarily be seen as mediators between God and humans in that they were responsible for the sacrifices offered in atonement for the transgressions of the people. Such was a sacred task, and one which should have been performed with scrupulous attention to the detail of the divine instructions. Whatever the exact nature of the transgression(s) of Nadab and Abihu, it is clear that they failed in this duty.

God is just, and we cannot doubt that God acted justly here. This is a reminder to all of the holiness of God, and that his worship, and the leading of such worship, should be suitably reverential.

The story of Nadab and Abihu cannot be brushed aside and treated as just a story about disobedient priests. The implications go far beyond that. In 1 Peter 2:9 we read:

> But you are a chosen people, a royal priesthood, a holy nation, God's special possession, that you may declare

> the praise of him who called you out of darkness into his wonderful light.

The people of God, the church, are here described as a 'royal priesthood'. We are to 'declare the praise of him who called you out of darkness into his wonderful light'. Our salvation is for the purpose of proclaiming praise to God. The events in Leviticus relating to Nadab and Abihu should concentrate our minds on the importance and centrality of true worship in our individual and church lives.

Rooker,[19] at this point in his commentary on Leviticus quotes appropriately from Calvin's comments on this text:

> If we reflect how holy a thing God's worship is, the enormity of the punishment will by no means offend us. Besides, it was necessary that their religion should be sanctified at its very commencement; for if God had suffered the sons of Aaron to transgress with impunity, they would have afterwards carelessly neglected the whole law. This, therefore, was the reason of such great severity, that the priests should anxiously watch against all profanation.

KORAH

Numbers 16:1-35

> Korah son of Izhar, the son of Kohath, the son of Levi, and certain Reubenites – Dathan and Abiram, sons of Eliab, and On son of Peleth – became insolent and rose up against Moses. With them were 250 Israelite men, well-known community leaders who had been appointed members of the council. They came as a group to oppose Moses and Aaron and said to them, 'You have gone too far! The whole community is holy, every one of them, and the Lord is with them. Why then do you set yourselves above the Lord's assembly?'

---

[19] Mark F. Rooker, *Leviticus*, NAC (Nashville: B & H, 2000), p.158.

When Moses heard this, he fell face down. Then he said to Korah and all his followers: 'In the morning the Lord will show who belongs to him and who is holy, and he will make that person come near him. The man he chooses he will cause to come near him. You, Korah, and all your followers are to do this: take censers and tomorrow put burning coals and incense in them before the Lord. The man the Lord chooses will be the one who is holy. You Levites have gone too far!'

Moses also said to Korah, 'Now listen, you Levites! Isn't it enough for you that the God of Israel has separated you from the rest of the Israelite community and brought you near himself to do the work at the Lord's tabernacle and to stand before the community and minister to them? He has brought you and all your fellow Levites near himself, but now you are trying to get the priesthood too. It is against the Lord that you and all your followers have banded together. Who is Aaron that you should grumble against him?'

Then Moses summoned Dathan and Abiram, the sons of Eliab. But they said, 'We will not come! Isn't it enough that you have brought us up out of a land flowing with mild and honey to kill us in the wilderness? And now you want to lord it over us! Moreover, you haven't brought us into a land flowing with mild and honey or given us an inheritance of fields and vineyards. Do you want to treat these men like slaves? No, we will not come!'

Then Moses became very angry and said to the Lord, 'Do not accept their offering. I have not taken so much as a donkey from them, nor have I wronged any of them.'

Moses said to Korah, 'You and all your followers are to appear before the Lord tomorrow – you and they and Aaron. Each man is to take his censer and put incense in it – 250 censers in all – and present it before the Lord. You and Aaron are to present your censers also.' So each of them took his censer, put burning coals and incense in it, and stood with Moses and Aaron at the entrance to the tent of meeting. When Korah had gathered all his followers in opposition to them at the entrance to the tent of meeting, the glory of the Lord appeared to the entire assembly. The Lord said to Moses and Aaron, 'Separate yourselves from this assembly so that I can put an end to them at once.'

But Moses and Aaron fell face down and cried out, 'O God, the God who gives breath to all living things, will you be angry with the entire assembly when only one man sins?

Then the Lord said to Moses, 'Say to the assembly, "Move away from the tents of Korah, Dathan and Abirham." '

Moses got up and went to Dathan and Abiram, and the elders of Israel followed him. He warned the assembly, 'Move back from the tents of these wicked men! Do not touch anything belonging to them, or you will be swept away because of all their sins.' So they moved away from the tens of Korah, Dathan and Abiram. Dathan and Abiram had come out and were standing with their wives, children and little ones at the entrances to their tents.

Then Moses said, 'This is how you will know that the Lord has sent me to do all these things and that it was not my idea: if these men die a natural death and suffer the fate of all mankind, then the Lord has not sent me. But if the Lord brings about something totally new, and the earth opens its mouth and swallows them, with everything that belongs to then, and they go down alive into the realm of the dead, then you will know that these men have treated the Lord with contempt.'

As soon as he had finished saying all this, the ground under them split apart and the earth opened its mouth and swallowed them and their households, and all those

> associated with Korah, together with their possessions. They went down alive to the realm of the dead, with everything they owned; the earth closed over them, and they perished and were gone from the community. At their cries, all the Israelites around them fled, shouting, 'The earth is going to swallow us too!'
>
> And fire came out from the Lord and consumed the 250 men who were offering the incense.

Moses' authority has already been threatened, and from within his own family no less, when his brother Aaron and his sister Miriam challenged his leadership in Numbers 12. Here is another challenge, this time from some Kohathites, and others from the tribe of Reuben. The Kohathites were of the tribe of Levi and had the responsibility for the sacred objects of the tabernacle, and here they are led by Korah, the son of Kohath. Reuben, the progenitor of the tribe named after him, was the eldest son of Jacob, with Leah as his mother. He is remembered for admirable acts, such as advising his brothers not to kill Joseph (Genesis 37:21), later returning to the cistern to release him (Genesis 37:29) and offering his two sons as a guarantee for the safety of his youngest brother Benjamin (Genesis 42:37). Nonetheless, his record is besmirched by him having sexual relations with his father's concubine Bilhah (Genesis 35:22).

Korah, the leader of the insurrection, clearly did not think that his position in the Israelite nation, albeit privileged, was suitably elevated for someone of his character. The motivation of the Reubenites is less obvious. The people, when they made camp, did so in an orderly and organised manner. Each tribe had their own allocated position in designated locations around the tabernacle. It has been suggested by Coakley[20] that the Reubenites may have been jealous of the privileged placement of the tribe of Judah within the camp, particularly as their ancestor was the firstborn, whilst Judah was the fourth son. That be as it may, the Kohathites and some of the Reubenites are in revolt against the leadership of Moses.

---

[20] James Coakley, in *The Moody Bible Commentary*, ed. Michael Rydelnik and Michael Vanlaningham (Chicago: Moody, 2014), p.237.

The rebels express their grievance in verse 3: '"You have gone too far! The whole community is holy, every one of them, and the Lord is with them. Why then do you set yourselves against the Lord's assembly?", This may sound not unreasonable at first sight, but the underlying motive is malignant. They are in essence saying that as the whole nation is holy, what right do Moses and Aaron have to assert authority over them? Why should they be the ones to tell others what to do? Although ostensibly they are questioning the right of the current leadership to direct operations, one might legitimately wonder about other covert reasons. For example, Allen[21] questions whether Korah has also been attempting to install himself as high priest (both Moses and Aaron would at this time have been in their eighties at least).

Moses challenges the opposition to a type of trial by ordeal in which the following morning each side would offer incense to the Lord, and 'the Lord will show who is his' (Numbers 16:5). Dathan and Abiram refuse to participate, for reasons that are not wholly clear.

Korah and his 250 followers turn up the next day with their censors. At this point 'the glory of the Lord appeared to the entire assembly' (16:19). Moses is told to instruct the people to move away from the tents of Korah, Dathan and Abiram, and this was obeyed. Moses then states that if the men died of natural causes, then he is not the leader chosen by God, but if the earth opens and swallows them up alive, then 'you will know that these men have treated the Lord with contempt' (16:30). The earth accordingly opened and swallowed Korah, his followers, and their possessions.

As is alluded to elsewhere in this book, motive cannot necessarily be seen as singular. There is often more than one motive, although the relative importance of each factor may vary. Even co-conspirators may not share the same motivators, or at least not in the same proportions. We have already seen that the Reubenites may have acted on a different rational basis from that of Korah. The latter would seem to have acted from a desire for self-aggrandizement. He may well have coveted the position of high priest, but it seems likely that underpinning that sinful desire was a personality consumed with

---

[21] Ronald B. Allen, *Genesis, Exodus, Leviticus, Numbers*, The Expositor's Bible Commentary, Vol. 2 (Grand Rapids: Zondervan, 1990), p.835.

pride. *He* was an important person. *He* deserved more than his current position in the pecking order (despite it being a significant and important function). He seems to have thought he could do Moses' and Aaron's jobs better than could they. He thought he was the better man for the job.

It is vitally important here to mark that the Israelite agitators were not just opposing the leadership status of Moses and Aaron. Their actions may at first glance be regarded as base and selfish, but their offences were much more profound than that. Moses and Aaron, their leaders were not placed in their positions by self-appointment or on the basis of an election by the Israelite people. Their leadership offices were by divine executive direction. Opposition to them therefore was an act of rebellion against God. Divine retribution was swift in coming.

In contrast to the insurrectionists, consider the character reference to Moses at the end of the book of Deuteronomy (34:10-12):

> Since then, no prophet has risen in Israel like Moses, whom the Lord knew face to face, who did all those signs and wonders the Lord sent him to do in Egypt – to Pharaoh and to all his officials and to his whole land. For no one has ever shown the mighty power or performed the awesome deeds that Moses did in the sight of all Israel.

What an epitaph!

UZZAH

2 Samuel 6:1-7

> David again brought together all the able young men of Israel – thirty thousand. He and all his men went to Baalah in Judah to bring up from there the ark of God, which is called by the Nae, the name of the Lord Almighty, who is enthroned between the cherubim on the ark. They set the ark of God on a new cart and brought it from the house of Abinadab, which was on the hill. Uzzah and Ahio, sons of Abinadab, were guiding

> the new cart with the ark of God on it, and Ahio was walking in front of it. David and all Israel were celebrating with all their might before the Lord, with castanets, harps, lyres, tambourines, rattles and cymbals. When they came to the threshing floor of Nakon, Uzzah reached out and took hold of the ark of God, because the oxen stumbled. The Lord's anger burned against Uzzah because of his irreverent act; therefore God struck him down, and he died there beside the ark of God.

David is king of Israel, and Jerusalem has recently been designated his capital city. He is aware that his kingship is not autonomous, but that rather, he is God's agent in a theocracy – it is God who holds ultimate authority over the nation, who are God's people. The desire to bring the ark of the covenant to Jerusalem can be seen as tacit acknowledgement of this reality. Although symbols are of important significance in today's world, it is easy for us to underestimate their importance in the ancient world where literacy was extremely limited, as were other forms of communication which we today take for granted.

Despite his laudable intention, it is clear that David has not done his homework. By placing the ark on a cart, the Torah instructions of Numbers 4:15, and 7:9 were being violated. The ark was to be *carried*, not transported on a vehicle. This error is recognised by David in 1 Chronicles 15:13 when he says, 'It was because you, the Levites, did not bring it up the first time that the Lord our God broke out in anger against us. We did not enquire of him about how to do it in the prescribed way'.

Nevertheless, the cart bearing the ark is wending its way towards Jerusalem. There is jubilation among the people at this historic event, joyous celebration with musical accompaniment. Unfortunately, the proceedings are not climaxed with the arrival of the cart in the capital city, but with disaster.

As can be seen from the passage of Scripture quoted above, Ahio is leading the procession, and his brother Uzzah is 'guiding' the cart containing the ark. Almost certainly (although it is not made explicit in Scripture), these men were Levites from the Kohath family, as this would be their duty under the provisions of Numbers 4:4-20.

As the procession progresses, the oxen stumble. Here the NASB rendering is worth noting: 'the oxen nearly upset *it*' (meaning the cart). Uzzah reaches out to steady the ark and protect it from harm. In his instinctive action he had neglected the words of Numbers 4:15:

> After Aaron and his sons have finished covering the holy furnishings and all the holy articles, and when the camp is ready to move, only then are the Kohathites to come and do the carrying. But they must not touch the holy things, or they will die. The Kohathites are to carry those things that are in the tent of meeting.

God immediately struck Uzzah down, and he died on the spot.

We are prone to think of Uzzah's abrupt death as being an unnecessarily draconian punishment (even despite its prescription in the Torah). Such an emotional response indicates not only a failure to respect the law of God, but also demonstrates a parsimonious view of the holiness of God (which will be explored in more detail at the end of this book).

Evans'[22] remarks serve as an apt conclusion to this salutary tale:

> The story of Uzzah's death is difficult for many modern Christians. But as noted above, Uzzah's actions did not respect God's holiness; he was aware of the dangerous nature of the ark and should have known better. Yet, God's reaction still seems harsh as Uzzah dies immediately for his transgression. Similarly, in the New Testament Ananias and Sapphira die immediately for their sin (Acts 5:1-11). These stories bother us because most of the time people do not die instantly for their sin, and it seems unfair. However, we must realize that the reason the vast majority of people do not die instantly for their transgression is due to God's patience and mercy. God is gracious and slow to anger. But his anger is real. God's delay in punishments should remind us of God's patience, but instead it often leads us to forget that we must take sin seriously.

[22] Paul S. Evans, *1-2 Samuel*, SGBC (Grand Rapids: Zondervan, 2018), p.355.

ANANIAS AND SAPPHIRA

Acts 5:1-11

Now a man named Ananias, together with his wife Sapphira, also sold a piece of property. With his wife's full knowledge he kept back part of the money for himself, but brought the rest and put it at the apostles' feet.

Then Peter said, "Ananias, how is it that Satan has so filled your heart that you have lied to the Holy Spirit and have kept for yourself some of the money you received for the land? Didn't it belong to you before it was sold? And after it was sold, wasn't the money at your disposal? What made you think of doing such a thing? You have not lied just to human beings but to God.'

When Ananias heard this, he fell down and died. And great fear seized all who heard what had happened. Then some young men came forward, wrapped up his body, and carried him out and buried him.

About three hours later his wife came in, not knowing what had happened. Peter asked her, 'Tell me, is this the price you and Ananias got for the land?'

'Yes,' she said, 'that is the price.'

Peter said to her, 'How could you conspire to test the Spirit of the Lord? Listen! The feet of the men who buried your husband are at the door, and they will carry you out also.'

At that moment she fell down at his feet and died. Then the young men came in and , finding her dead, carried her out and buried her beside her husband. Great fear seized the whole church and all who heard about these events.

The story of Ananias and Sapphira is a frightening one, and salutary in its import for Christians. As can be readily appreciated from the last section of the Scripture passage reproduced above, it certainly caused fear among other Christians, and indeed among other people who heard of these events.

First, it is necessary to consider the context of this event. In the two verses preceding those quoted above we read,

> Joseph, a Levite from Cyprus, whom the apostles called Barnabas (which means 'son of encouragement'), sold a field he owned and brought the money and put it at the apostles' feet. (Acts 4:36-37)

It would seem likely that the couple had seen the example of Barnabas, and doubtless also the respect and gratitude he likely gained from this by others in the Christian fellowship. The culture of the time was different from that which pertains in the Western world today. There was an honour/shame culture, and Ananias and Sapphira would have likely desired the honour accorded to Barnabas for his actions, despite him unlikely to have been so motivated. They are likely to have been young in the faith and not yet fully integrated into Christian mores. One can readily appreciate that they too wanted to be esteemed in the eyes of their new associates in Christ, and so they emulate Barnabas by selling some property and donating the money to the cause. So far so good.

But Ananias and Sapphira do not give all the proceeds to the church, although they purport to do so. They covertly retain some of the proceeds for their own use. It is clear from the biblical record that Peter is aware of this subterfuge when he speaks to Ananias in verses three and four. It is likewise clear that there was no obligation on Ananias to give all the proceeds from the sale when Peter says to him, 'Didn't it belong to you before it was sold? And after it was sold wasn't the money at your disposal?' It is also evident that Ananias had planned his actions in collusion with his wife, because when Sapphira arrives three hours later, upon being questioned by Peter, she too attests that the donated money comprised the exact amount of the proceeds from the sale.

Both husband and wife collapse and die after their discussions with Peter.

The initial reaction of some may be to think that Ananias and Sapphira were unfairly treated – that the punishment didn't fit the crime – that they were dealt with much too severely. One might suspect that such an attitude might in part relate to the absence or virtual absence of church discipline in many churches today. Were they dealt with appropriately? We must first recognise that their deaths were not the result of any disciplinary measures taken by the church of their time, but rather the consequence of a sovereign act of God. Before returning to the consequences of their actions, we should first have a better understanding of their offence, their sin.

As Thomas[23] points out, the word used by Peter translated 'kept back' in the NIV is *enosphisato* in the Greek text and is only used in one other place in the New Testament, in Titus 2:10, where in the NIV it is translated as 'steal'. Thomas thus concludes that:

> It must therefore be assumed that Ananias and Sapphira had entered into some kind of understanding with the church *before* the sale transpired. The judgement was not because Ananias had not given the whole of the proceeds as such; it was because he lied to the apostles as to the amount he had made on the sale. He effectively *lied to the Holy Spirit*.
>
> Ananias had lied not simply "to men but to God" (Acts 5:4). The magnitude of his sin lies in this fact: Ananias sinned *against God*. In the strictest sense, he "robbed God" (Malachi 3:8).

Looked at this way, any residual sympathy for Ananias and Sapphira is rapidly dissipated.

It is also worthy of noting, as Thomas does, that the word *enosphisato* is found only once in the Septuagint (the Greek translation of the Old Testament used by many Christians of that

[23] Derek W. H. Thomas, *Acts*, REC (Phillipsburg: P & R, 2011), p.123.

day), and it is used of Achan's actions in taking items from Jericho, resulting in his execution.

When we think through matters carefully, we can see that Ananias and Sapphira were guilty of the following sins:

1. Lying (to man and God)
2. Robbery (of God)
3. Hypocrisy (spiritual deception)

As Hughes[24] points out, 'Spiritual deception is heinous to God! When we lie to believers, we are not lying to them but to the Lord!'

The fear engendered in the early church by these events is hardly surprising. The church would have been reminded of the holiness of God. As Thomas[25] further comments,

> God is to be loved, but he is also to be respected. In what appears too often as a therapeutic concern for affirming our status as children in God's family when we conceive of God, we are often far too relaxed. We are the children of God by faith in Jesus Christ with all the rights and privileges of sons. But this assurance of our status as sons should not lead us into a reckless disregard for holiness and commitment on our part.

This episode in the life of the nascent Christian church is a potent reminder of the importance of church discipline. The Reformers held to three cardinal principles for the church:

1. The administration of the sacraments
2. The propagation of the gospel
3. Church discipline

The church today firmly holds to the first two, but there is all too frequently an ignoring or sidelining of the third component.

---

[24] R. Kent Hughes, *Acts*, PTW (Wheaton: Crossway, 1996), p.78

[25] Ibid, p.127.

In a characteristically perceptive comment on this passage, the late Professor Bruce[26] commented that,

> The story of Ananias is to the book of Acts what the story of Achan is to the book of Joshua. In both narratives an act of deceit interrupts the victorious progress of the people of God.

Discussion

From the foregoing, it can readily be appreciated that whereas the final judgement in eschatological times is definitive, this does not preclude God, in his justice, acting decisively in this life. These cases are those in which egregious sin could no longer be tolerated by a holy God.

In Genesis 1:31 we read that 'God saw all that he had made, and it was very good.' Then, in Genesis 3 there is the fall. By Genesis 6:5, 'The Lord saw how great the wickedness of the human race had become on the earth, and that every inclination of the thoughts of the human heart was only evil all the time.' God decided to extinguish human life, with the exception of Noah and his family. Although according to Genesis 6:9, 'Noah was a righteous man, blameless among the people of his time, and he walked faithfully with God', as Tremper Longman III[27] points out, he was righteous in that he obeyed the commands of God. He had a sinful nature as did the rest of mankind, but God chose him in an act of grace. Noah was saved from the flood by the grace of God, just as Christians today are only saved from eternal punishment by God's grace.

The offence committed by Nadab and Abihu is still not wholly clear, despite centuries of debate by both Jewish and Christian commentators. It is difficult to know precisely the nature of the 'unauthorised fire', or 'strange fire' as it is sometimes called. Rooker[28] lists the four most commonly proposed explanations for their offence:

---

[26] F. F. Bruce, *The Book of the Acts*, NICNT (Grand Rapids: Eerdmans, 1988), p.102.
[27] Tremper Longman III, *Genesis*, STOGBC (Grand Rapids: Zondervan, 2016), p.117.
[28] Mark F. Rooker, *Leviticus*, NAC (Nashville: B & H, 2000), p.157.

1. Penetrating too far into the sanctuary
2. Offering unauthorized coals from outside the temple area
3. Offering incense that did not contain the proper ingredients
4. Offering incense at the wrong time of day

Additionally, although the biblical text does not say they were inebriated at the time, the warning in verses 8-9 to priests against the consumption of alcohol before entering the tent of meeting has suggested this possibility to some as an explanation.

The offence in the case of Korah and his band of rebels is crystal clear. Not only were they rebelling against the leadership of Moses and Aaron, but they were also rebelling against God who had appointed them leaders. Their fate was inevitable.

Uzzah violated a divine command which was designed to protect God's holiness from being defiled.

It can readily be appreciated that the first three of these shocking instances where God's wrath has been spectacularly made manifest have common features:

1. Gross sin. God's commands have been flouted with impunity.
2. More than one individual was involved. In the case of the flood, whole of humanity, in the case of Korah, an unknown number, and two in the case of the priests.
3. In each case, God had made his stipulations clear.
4. In each case there was what we might refer to as a 'faithful remnant' who were saved. In the flood, Noah and his family survived to repopulate the earth. Of the priestly family, Aaron's two remaining sons, Eleazer and Ithamar would continue the priestly line. In the third case, most of the Israelites survived.

In the fourth case, that of Uzzah, points one, three, and four can be considered to apply.

The cases of Ananias and Sapphira are found in the New Testament and are thus in the age of the New as opposed to the Old Covenant. Nevertheless, what constitutes sin is unchanged. Their offences of lying, robbery, and hypocrisy have already been noted. These too can appropriately be seen as acts of rebellion against God.

The comparisons with our own day are obvious. God demands justice for sin. Jesus bore the penalty for sin (the sins of believers) at Calvary, and Christians today can be looked on as a 'faithful remnant' compared with the rest of the earth's population.

The account of Korah's rebellion has a clear and direct application to the church of today. It is not uncommon for there to be dissent of varying degrees in congregations in respect of the views of the leadership. Sometimes there are legitimate grounds for this, and those involved must seek solutions without acting improperly. Nevertheless, as Sprinkle[29] pertinently points out, different church members have different functions, as Paul indicates in 1 Corinthians 12:12-26, and also later in verses 28-29 he gives examples of this differentiation. In medical practice it is easy to spot differentiation of function. I am a retired forensic psychiatrist, whereas other doctors work as general practitioners, physicians, and surgeons, amongst other specialities. Some are still in the training grades, whereas others have consultant status. Church members should be aware of their own area of gifting, and expertise, whether it be academic or practical, and not seek to influence, or have influence over, issues on which they have no qualifications or experience to pontificate.

In all these cases we see heinous rebellion against God and its inevitable calamitous consequences. In our day we recognise that humankind continues to rebel against God, and that the eternal consequences are frightful. Such should prove a powerful impetus to obeying the Lord's injunction in Matthew 28:19-20 to 'go and make disciples of all nations, baptising them in the name of the Father and of the Son and of the Holy Spirit, and teaching them to obey everything I have commanded you'.

---

[29] Joe M. Sprinkle, *Leviticus and Numbers*, TTT (Grand Rapids: Baker, 2015), p.285.

Chapter Four
MASS SLAUGHTER

Introduction

The deliberate killing of all or part of an ethnic, racial, religious, or national group is known by the term genocide. Although first defined by the United Nations in 1948, the concept has been practised for millennia. Today, we probably think first of the Holocaust, the Nazi genocide of around six million Jews during the second world war. Some may be surprised to learn that more people were killed in genocidal acts in the twentieth century than in any other century in history. Events such as the Darfur, Rwandan, Bangladesh, Armenian, and Cambodian genocides are often not widely recognised.

At the time of writing the war in Ukraine has commenced its second year. More than 7,000 civilians have lost their lives so far, most from explosive weapons such as heavy artillery, multiple launch rocket systems, missile and air strikes, at least some of these apparently indiscriminate in their targeting. At the recent World Economic Forum in Davos, Switzerland, a Ukrainian presidential aide stated that his government had registered 80,000 crimes committed by the Russian invaders. He reiterated calls for a special international tribunal to try Russia and reparations for the destruction caused by the invasion. Although events in Ukraine may not at this stage amount to genocide in the formal understanding of the word, they are a reminder that such an atrocity is not so far divorced from modern life as we might think.

Some Christians flinch when they come across passages such as 1 Samuel 15:1-3:

> Samuel said to Saul, 'I am the one the Lord sent to anoint you king over his people Israel; so listen now to the message from the Lord. This is what the Lord Almighty says: "I will punish the Amalekites for what they did to Israel when they waylaid them as they came up from Egypt. Now go, attack the Amalekites and totally destroy all that belongs to them. Do not spare them; put to death men and women, children and infants, cattle and sheep, camels and donkeys."

The thought of widespread killing of a nation of people of whatever age and sex (and especially children) is met with revulsion by many and today, for some, the deliberate ending of the lives of livestock might attract similar sentiments.

Others, who may have enjoyed Bob Marley's rendition of 'Rivers of Babylon' in their younger years, when reading Psalm 137 (from which it was derived) may well blench when they come to the sentiments of the final verse:

> Happy is the one who seizes your infants and dashes them against the rocks.

They may be somewhat mollified here by the quote from Alden found in 'The Moody Bible Commentary'[30]:

> It is likely that the psalmist was not actually speaking of little ones in a literal sense, but rather, the descendants of Babylon as a whole, that is, all the citizens of "the wicked mother Babylon" (Alden, *Psalms: Songs of Discipleship*, 3:85).

In the New Testament we read Jesus' words in Matthew 5:43-44, where he says:

> 'You have heard that it was said, "Love your neighbour and hate your enemy." But I tell you, love your enemies

[30] *The Moody Bible Commentary*, ed. Michael Rydelnick and Michael Vanlaningham (Chicago: Moody, 1914), p.872

> and pray for those who persecute you, that you may be children of your Father in heaven.'

Again, in Luke 6:27-36, when talking about how we should treat our enemies, Jesus says:

> 'But to you who are listening I say: love your enemies, do good to those who hate you, bless those who curse you, pray for those who ill-treat you. If someone slaps you on one cheek, turn to them the other also. If someone takes your coat, do not withhold your shirt from them. Give to everyone who asks you, and if anyone takes what belongs to you, do not demand it back. Do to others as you would have them do to you.
>
> If you love those who love you, what credit is that to you? Even sinners love those who love them. And if you do good to those who are good to you, what credit is that to you? Even sinners do that. And if you lend to those from whom you expect repayment, what credit is that to you? Even sinners lend to sinners, expecting to be repaid in full. But love your enemies, do good to them, and lend to them without expecting to get anything back. Then your reward will be great, and you will be children of the Most High, because he is kind to the ungrateful and wicked. Be merciful, just as your Father is merciful.'

Biblical passages such as these, without careful analytical consideration are prone to engender the thought that the God of the Old Testament is a different God from the Father of Jesus. We are so attuned to the mantra 'God is love', that we tend to neglect other characteristics inherent in the character of God. The love of God, for example, should be balanced with an appreciation of God's justice, and the need for it. We should emphatically not fall into the error of the well-known second century heretic Marcion who, amongst other false teachings, asserted that the Gods of the Old and New Testaments were different Gods.[31]

---

[31] *A Dictionary of Early Christian Beliefs*, ed. David W. Bercot (Peabody: Hendrickson, 1998), p.419.

Cowles[32] has summarised the situation as he sees it:

> How do we harmonize the warrior God of Israel with the God of love incarnate in Jesus? How can we reconcile God's instructions to "utterly destroy" the Canaanites in the Old Testament with Jesus' command to "love your enemies" in the New Testament? The short answer is: with great difficulty.

But many disagree with Cowles. Although Lalleman[33] accepts that 'Verses such as Deuteronomy 7:1.2 and 20:17 *are* difficult', and it is difficult to disagree from this opinion, others have provided insights into the Old Testament texts which not only assist in our understanding, but also in the modulation of our hitherto held attitudes. These will be addressed, albeit in brief, in the discussion which follows this section of the book.

SODOM AND GOMORRAH

Genesis 19:23-29

> By the time Lot reached Zoar, the sun had risen over the land. Then the Lord rained down burning sulphur on Sodom and Gomorrah – from the Lord out of the heavens. Thus he overthrew those cities and the entire plain, destroying all those living in the cities – and also the vegetation in the land. But Lot's wife looked back, and she became a pillar of salt.
>
> Early the next morning Abraham got up and returned to the place where he had stood before the Lord. He looked down towards Sodom and Gomorrah, towards all the land of the plain, and he saw dense smoke rising from the land, like smoke from a furnace.
>
> So when God destroyed the cities of the plain, he remembered Abraham, and he brought lot out of the

---

[32] C. S. Cowles, in *Show Them No Mercy, Four Views on God and Canaanite Genocide,* ed. Stanley N. Gundry (Grand Rapids: Zondervan, 2003), p.14

[33] Hetty Lalleman, *Celebrating the Law?* (Milton Keynes: Paternoster, 2016), p.91.

> catastrophe that overthrew the cities where Lot had lived.

The divine destruction of Sodom and Gomorrah is well known, even to those outside of Christian circles. That those cities were centres for sinful behaviour is likewise recognised, as is the derivation of the word 'sodomy'.

The above passage of Scripture documents their destruction, but it is appropriate here to recall those events which led up to that fateful day.

Abraham, the famous patriarch left his home in Ur and left for Canaan on the instructions of God. On the journey, the family initially settled in Haran, where Terah, Abraham's father died. Abraham then sets out for Canaan with his wife, and Lot, his nephew (Gen. 11:27-12:5). Eventually they settle between Bethel and Ai, about 10 miles north of Jerusalem. By this time they have such large numbers of livestock that the land cannot support them all (Gen. 13:5-6). They decide to separate, and Abraham gives Lot first choice of future location. Lot plumps for the fertile Jordan valley and lives in Sodom. There, foreign kings sacked Sodom and Gomorrah, and Lot is taken prisoner before being rescued by Abraham.

The events of the biblical passage above follow hugely significant episodes in the life of Abraham. God has covenanted with him in Genesis 15 and 17. The Lord then appears to Abraham with two angelic beings and promises a son to him (an heir!) and his wife Sarah. At this time Abraham is very old and Sarah is past the time of child-bearing (Genesis18:1-15).

It is at this meeting that the Lord says to Abraham (Genesis 18:20-21):

> 'The outcry against Sodom and Gomorrah is so great and their sin so grievous that I will go down and see if what they have done is as bad as the outcry that has reached me. If not, I will know.'

Abraham clearly knows that his nephew is residing in Sodom, and also of its unenviable reputation for debauchery. He clearly wants to save the city from what appears to be the inevitable judgement of God. He attempts to bargain with God in a way perhaps reminiscent of haggling for goods in an oriental souk, or even with a car salesman today. He pleads with God to spare the city if fifty righteous individuals can be found there. Having been successful in this application, and obviously far from confident that this quota will be fulfilled, he continues to whittle the required numbers down until God agrees that even if only ten righteous people can be found, he will not destroy it (Genesis 18:22-33).

God leaves, but the two angels proceed to Sodom. There, Lot is in the city gateway. He greets them and offers them overnight hospitality at his house. Although they initially decline and state they will spend the night in the city square, Lot's entreaties overcome their protestations and they accompany him home and have a meal. At this stage a crowd of men, indeed,

> all the men from every part of the city of Sodom - both young and old-surrounded the house. They called to Lot, 'Where are the men who came to you tonight? Bring them out to us so that we can have sex with them.'
> (Genesis 19:4-5)

To our surprise Lot offers his virgin daughters to the men for sex, but it is the angelic beings they are after, and they refuse to be deterred from their objective. The angels strike the male crowd with blindness so that they cannot find the door to the house.

The angels then tell Lot to collect his family and leave the city because the place is to be destroyed. The angels guide Lot, his wife, and his daughters safely out of the city. Lot and his daughters successfully escape, but his wife lingers, looks back, and is turned into a 'pillar of salt'.

We don't know whether Lot's wife was a native of Sodom or not. His two daughters are shortly to sin by inducing intoxication in him, sleeping with him, and subsequently bearing male children who are to father the Moabites and the Ammonites, both of whom were to be at enmity with the Israelites in the future.

Catastrophe hit the earth at the time of the flood. Here there is calamity for Sodom and Gomorrah. On both occasions the earth's population was going about their daily business. Luke 17:26-30 reminds us that the situation will be the same at our Lord's second coming:

> Just as it was in the days of Noah, so also will it be in the days of the Son of Man. People were eating, drinking, marrying and being given in marriage up to the day Noah entered the ark. Then the flood came and destroyed them all.
>
> It was the same in the days of Lot. People were eating and drinking, buying and selling, planting and building. But the day Lot left Sodom, fire and sulphur rained down from heaven and destroyed them all.
>
> It will be just like this on the day the Son of Man is revealed.

THE TRANSJORDAN TRIBES

Deuteronomy 3:1-6

> Next we turned and went up along the road towards Bashan, and Og king of Bashan with his whole army marched out to meet us in battle at Edrei. The Lord said to me, 'Do not be afraid of him, for I have delivered him into your hands, along with his whole army and his land. Do to him what you did to Sihon king of the Amorites, who reigned in Heshbon.'
>
> So the Lord our God also gave into our hands Og king of Bashan and all his army. We struck them down, leaving no survivors. At that time we took all his cities. There was not one of the sixty cities that we did not take from them – the whole region of Argob, Og's kingdom in Bashan. All these cities were fortified with high walls and with gates and bars, and there were also a great many unwalled villages. We completely destroyed them, as we had done with Sihon king of Heshbon, destroying every city – men, women and children.

This passage is part of a lengthy discourse by Moses, documenting the progress of the Israelites in their journey to the promised land. Moses is speaking towards the end of the years of wilderness wanderings, when the Israelites were camped in Moab, just across the River Jordan from the promised land of Canaan. Moses would shortly die, and his successor, Joshua, would lead the people to their new home. Here, Moses rehearses, in more detail than is found in the Book of Numbers, the journey around Edom to their current location, including the defeat of the kings Og and Sihon.

Towards the end of the 40-year trek to the promised land, Israel asked the Edomites for permission to traverse their land, offering payment for any food and water consumed. This was denied, and Moses thus led them on a route heading north, round Edom and towards Moab and the place where the nation would cross the River Jordan. In the passage above, they have reached Heshbon. This site is still present today, in Jordan, and is known as Hesban. There they fought Sihon, the king of the Amorites with conspicuous success. They then went to Bashan where they were attacked by King Og and his army at a place called Edrei. This is thought to be the site of Der'a in what is now Syria. Later, this area was to be part of the land assigned to the tribe of Manasseh in the allocation of the land, determined by lot, following the fighting for conquest of the land (Joshua 17). King Og and his military forces are also vanquished by the Israelites.

The main interest here, from the perspective of this chapter, however, is the last sentence quoted above: 'And we devoted them to destruction every city, men, women, and children'. The peoples of Kings Og and Bashan are recorded as being annihilated regardless of age and sex. The Hebrew word used here is *herem*, which is used elsewhere in the conquest for total destruction and will figure more prominently in the discussion at the end of this section of the book.

JERICHO

Joshua 6:15-21

> On the seventh day, they got up at daybreak and marched round the city seven times in the same manner, except that on that day they circled the city seven times. The seventh time round, when the priests sounded the

> trumpet blast, Joshua commanded the army, 'Shout! For the Lord has given you the city! The city and all that is in it are to be devoted to the Lord. Only Rahab the prostitute and all who are with her in her house shall be spared, because she hid the spies we sent. But keep away from the devoted things, so that you will not bring about your own destruction by taking any of them. Otherwise you will make the camp of Israel liable to destruction and bring trouble on it. All the silver and gold and the articles of bronze and iron are sacred to the Lord and must go into his treasury.'
>
> When the trumpets sounded, the army shouted, and at the sound of the trumpet, when the men gave a loud shout, the wall collapsed; so everyone charged straight in, and they took the city. They devoted the city to the Lord and destroyed with the sword every living thing in it – men and women, young and old, cattle, sheep and donkeys.

The nation of Israel has crossed the Jordan into the promised land. The expectations of the people would have been high. After 40 years in the waiting room of the wilderness they had finally arrived! Their leader, Joshua, had assured them before crossing the river that 'the living God is among you and that he will certainly drive out before you the Canaanites, Hitttites, Hivites, Perizzites, Girgashites, Amorites and Jebusites' (Joshua 3:10). After crossing, they set up memorial stones so that future generations would remember the miracle of crossing the Jordan on dry ground. This has more than an echo of the crossing of the Red (or Reed) Sea some forty years earlier, and significantly this too was at the same time of year – Passover. Additionally, the males were circumcised. No circumcisions appear to have been performed during the wanderings in the desert. The first Passover was celebrated in the promised land. At the end of Joshua 5 there is a remarkable encounter. Joshua sees a man in front of him with a drawn sword. The figure identifies himself as 'commander of the army of the Lord' (Joshua 5:14). Joshua is told to 'Take off your sandals, for the place where you are standing is holy' (Joshua 5:15). There has been considerable debate as to the identity of this figure, whether it was an angel, or a theophany (an appearance of God to human beings) and, if the latter, whether it was the preincarnate Christ. Nevertheless, this event has a clear parallel with Moses' commissioning at the 'burning bush' episode in Exodus 3. In particular, the reference to holy ground on both occasions will be noted. Joshua himself would have recognised this as a sign that God was with him, just as he had been with Moses.

Having crossed the Jordan, the river flow resumes, there is no way back, and the city of Jericho is blocking the way forward. It constituted a formidable obstacle, sitting on a mound of earth, with strong walls and a spring providing fresh water, and was occupied, at least largely, by soldiers. The Israelites had no experience of siege warfare, and in any case, were unequipped for it. God told Joshua to march round the city with his soldiers together with seven priests with trumpets preceding the ark. This was to happen for six days in a row, and on the seventh the priests were to blow their trumpets, accompanied by a loud shout from the rest of the procession. This was to result in the collapse of the walls, and thus the conquering of the city.

And so it did.

And that is where the Sunday School story usually ends. We, on the other hand, are here primarily concerned with the last sentence of the passage quoted above. Every living thing in the city was destroyed – 'men and women, young and old, cattle, sheep and donkeys'. Before turning to this specifically, it should be remembered that one individual, Rahab, and her household were excluded from this edict. Rahab was a prostitute living in Jericho who had hidden two Israelite spies before their army had approached the city, and sent the officers directed to arrest them on a wild goose chase, thus permitting their escape. As an incidental issue, it is worth noting here that Rahab appears in the genealogy of Christ (Matthew 1:5).

To our modern-day ears, the killing of all the inhabitants of the city, men, women, and children sounds monstrous and abhorrent. Yet, as is often the case, things are not as straightforward as they might first appear. Again, readers are referred to views presented in the discussion at the end of this section of the book.

AI

Joshua 8:18-29

Then the Lord said to Joshua, 'Hold out towards Ai the javelin that is in your hand, for into your hand I will deliver the city.' So Joshua held out towards the city the javelin that was in his hand. As soon as he did this, the men in the ambush rose quickly from their position and rushed forward. They entered the city and captured it and quickly set it on fire.

The men of Ai looked back and saw the smoke of the city rising up into the sky, but they had no chance to escape in any direction; the Israelites who had been fleeing towards the wilderness had turned back against their pursuers. For when Joshua and all Israel saw that the ambush had taken the city and that smoke was going up from the city, they turned round and attacked the men of Ai. Those in the ambush also came out of the city against them, so that they were caught in the middle, with Israelites on both sides. Israel cut them down, leaving them neither survivors nor fugitives. But they took the king of Ai alive and brought him to Joshua.

When Israel had finished killing all the men of Ai in the fields and in the wilderness where they had chased them, and when every one of them had been put to the sword, all the Israelites returned to Ai and killed those who were in it. Twelve thousand men and women fell that day – all the people of Ai. For Joshua did not draw back the hand that held out his javelin until he had destroyed all who lived in Ai. But Israel did carry off for themselves the livestock and plunder of this city, as the Lord had instructed Joshua.

So Joshua burned Ai and made it a permanent heap of ruins, a desolate place to this day. He impaled the body of the king of Ai on a pole and left it there until evening. At sunset, Joshua ordered them to take the body from the pole and throw it down at the entrance of the city gate.

> And they raised a large pile of rocks over it, which remains to this day.

It is helpful to be reminded of the events which led up to the events recounted above. After the stunning victory at Jericho, mediated by God's miraculous activity, the divine prohibition on booty was broken by Achan who plundered silver, gold, and a Babylonian robe. These were items which should have been devoted to God and were thus pillaged in direct contravention of God's command. This was not simple theft. The covenantal relationship between God and the people of Israel was broken. Here it must be remembered that at that period in time there was a different culture to that which tends to pertain today. There was a much stronger feeling of community then, as opposed to the emphasis on the individual today. Israelites in this sense were not individuals with their own sense of identity, rather their identity was subsumed under the nation of Israel. Being aware of this assists in understanding why God stated that, 'Israel has sinned; they have violated my covenant, which I have commanded them to keep'(Joshua 7:11). Achan's sin, the covenant-breaking sin of one Israelite, had infected the whole nation. Israel as a whole had indeed broken the covenant with God. Achan, significantly, was thus executed by 'all Israel' (Joshua 7:25), but not before damage had been done.

Following their triumph at Jericho, Israel went on to attack the city of Ai. It is worth noting here that 'Ai' means ruin. It thus seems likely that Ai was a makeshift fort based on existing ruins. The Israelites appear to have been confident of victory, their expectations doubtless bolstered by the events at Jericho. They attacked, took casualties, and their confidence vanished. It is at this point that Joshua approaches God, is told of the transgression by Israel, and Achan is identified and stoned. Atonement is thus made for the sin of Israel, and God instructs them to attack Ai, saying, 'You shall do to Ai and its king as you did to Jericho and its king, except that you may carry off their plunder and livestock for yourselves. Set an ambush behind the city' (Joshua 8:2). Note here that, as opposed to the attack on Jericho, the Israelites could keep the plunder for themselves rather than devoting it to God.

Careful planning is translated into effective action, and the passage above commences during the successful defeat of Ai. Other than the king of Ai, none of the inhabitants survived. The city was burned. As can be seen from the passage at the beginning of this chapter, the king's survival was only temporary. He was executed and his body placed on a pole for all to see. At sunset, in accordance with Deuteronomic law (Deuteronomy 21:22-23), it was removed.

Once again, as at Jericho, we have the annihilation of all of the inhabitants of the city. Again, this will be further addressed in the discussion section at the end of this chapter.

Although the point will not be laboured here, it should be noted that the stories of the conquering of Jericho and Ai are a reminder of the crucial importance of obeying divine commands, and of the consequences of non-compliance.

Discussion

The subject of genocide in the Bible is a complex one, and cannot be exhaustively covered in a volume such as this. There are many books which deal with this subject in a relatively straightforward manner, and they can be consulted for more detailed discussion.

1 Chronicles 2:7 reads as follows:

> The son of Karmi:
> Achar[34], who brought trouble on Israel by violating the ban on taking devoted things.

Some may be puzzled over the use of the term 'the ban', and it only appears on this occasion in the NIV. In other translations (for example, the NASB), it is employed more frequently. It is used to translate the Hebrew word *herem*, often translated as 'devoting to destruction'. As Evans puts it, 'The ban meant to utterly devote something to God (i.e., devote it to destruction), to annihilate or exterminate'.[35]

[34] Achar is called Achan in the Book of Joshua.
[35] Paul S. Evans, *1-2 Samuel*, TSOGC (Grand Rapids: Zondervan, 2018), p.162.

In Deuteronomy 20:16-18 we learn that prior to crossing the River Jordan into the promised land, the Israelites were instructed by God through Moses to apply the ban to the population there:

> However, in the cities of the nations the Lord your God is giving you as an inheritance, do not leave alive anything that breathes. Completely destroy them – the Hittites, Amorites, Canaanites, Perizzites, Hivites and Jebusites – as the Lord your God has commanded you. Otherwise, they will teach you to follow all the detestable things they do in worshipping their gods, and you will sin against the Lord your God.

It is clear that the rationale underpinning this instruction is the danger of the Israelites being led into idolatry. Nevertheless, this might not provide sufficient basis for some readers for their destruction. Further explanation is to be found in Deuteronomy 7:1-6:

> When the Lord your God brings you into the land you are entering to possess and drives out before you many nations – the Hittites, Girgashites, Amorites, Canaanites, Perizzites, Hivites and Jebusites, seven nations larger and stronger than you – and when the Lord your God has delivered them over to you and you have defeated them, then you must destroy them totally. Make no treaty with them, and show them no mercy. Do not intermarry with them. Do not give your daughters to their sons or take their daughters for your sons, for they will turn your children away from following me to serve other gods, and the Lord's anger will burn against you and will quickly destroy you. This is what you are to do to them: break down their altars, smash their sacred stones, cut down their Asherah poles and burn their idols in the fire. For you are a people holy to the Lord your God. The Lord your God has chosen you out of all the peoples of the earth to be his people, his treasured possession.

Coakley[36] makes several relevant observations on this passage:

---

[36] James Coakley, in *The Moody Bible Commentary*, ed. Michael Rydelnik and Michael Vanlaningham (Chicago: Moody, 2014). P.279.

1. All are sinners and hence under God's judgement. It is only by the mercy of God that anyone lives.
2. Deuteronomy 7:10 implies that these nations hated God – they were not neutral bystanders.
3. God had been patient with these nations for hundreds of years, and had delayed their denouement until this point in time (Genesis 15:16, where the word 'Amorites' probably designates the whole population of Canaan, as it can elsewhere).[37]
4. The existence of these peoples with their pagan practices risked the infection of the Israelites with their false beliefs and practices.

It is only by having a right appreciation of the holiness of God that we can appreciate his commands here. God detests sin. Mankind is sinful. It is only by his sovereign grace that we continue to exist on earth at all. When looked at through this lens, we do not view a God who is malign and vindictive, but one who is forbearing and patient with those humans who constantly sin against his righteous commands. It is important to remember that God had not acted in judgement against the Canaanites for a very prolonged period, despite their flagrant and perpetual sin.

We return to Cowles' comment, reproduced in the introduction to this section[38]. We might suspect a degree of irony here, but the issue he raises is indubitably one which troubles some Christians today and cannot be neglected. Only brief consideration can be afforded here. Readers who wish to pursue this matter in more detail are referred to the book from which the quotation is sourced. One initial point is that of Merrill[39], from the same book, who writes, 'One must quickly reaffirm, however, that the genocide sanctioned by Scripture was unique to its time, place, and circumstances'. These circumstances have been alluded to above. The fate of the Canaanites was an act of God acting in righteousness against sin. It should not be forgotten that some comparison can be made with the final

---

[37] Kenneth A. Mathews, *Genesis 11:27-50:26*, NAC (Nashville: B & H, 2005), p.175.
[38] C.S. Cowles, in *Show Them No Mercy, Four Views on God and Canaanite Genocide*, ed. Stanley N. Gundry (Grand Rapids: Zondervan, 2003), p.14.
[39] Eugene H. Merrill, in *Show Them No Mercy*, ed. Stanley N. Gundry (Grand Rapids: Zondervan, 2003), p.94.

judgement when complete resolution of rebellion against God will be made.

Nevertheless, we must balance the above with the views of Hess[40] and others. The command in Deuteronomy 20 is to destroy *cities*, which he interprets as forts which would have had a limited population, while the local population, living in the surrounding area would have likely fled to the hills at the approach of the Israelites. The fort would be where the ruler, the houses of the elite, the temples, the barracks and accommodation for the horses would be located. The masses would have lived in hamlets outside of the walls. It is the *city* which opposes God. On the basis of this understanding, the Israelites did not commit genocide. If this was indeed the case, where did all the Canaanites, who were subsequently to lead Israel astray, come from?

He also makes insightful comment on the controversial text of Joshua 6:21:

> They devoted the city to the Lord and destroyed with the sword every living thing in it – men and women, young and old, cattle, sheep and donkeys.

Although this might sound like genocide, Hess avers that the reference in the Hebrew text to men and women is a stereotypical phrase meaning 'everyone'. This would be everyone in the city or fort. It is *not* saying that non-combatants were killed. He suggests that the number of soldiers within Jericho (which was not large) might have been of the order of around 100.

Stone[41] notes that 'the rhetoric of extreme destruction and annihilation of all life likely reflects the fixed idioms of ancient military jargon'. He adds, 'In essence, any decisive victory finds expression in the most extreme language of annihilation, even if followed almost immediately by statements of the tributes to be

---

[40] Richard S. Hess. An excellent and thought-provoking lecture given at Biola University can be found on U Tube ('Did God command Joshua and Israel to commit genocide?').

[41] Lawson G. Stone, in *Ancient Israel's History*, ed.by Bill T. Arnold and Reichard S. Hess (Grand Rapids: Baker Academic, 2014), p.159-160.

levied on the (presumably dead!) population.' He also makes an oft missed point when he states:

> The book of Joshua actually stresses the killing of the "kings" far more strongly than the destruction of the cities themselves. The book does not report the Israelites attacking any Canaanite peasant villages or settlements or any encampment of pastoralists, an odd omission if the text really sought to report annihilation of the entire population. Only three cities are actually said to have been destroyed: Jericho, Ai, and Hazor (cf. Joshua 11:13). The list of towns in Joshua 12 does not claim that the towns were destroyed, or even assaulted. Reports of capture, not destruction, of Lachish, Eglon, Hebron, and Debir do appear in Joshua 10:29-39. These emphasise the killing of the city rulers. The list notwithstanding, Joshua 10 devotes its primary attention to the conspiracy of the five kings, their flight, imprisonment, and execution. Joshua 12 claims that "one king" in each town was killed. The kings of Canaan appear as the principal targets.

Tellingly, Lawson also goes on to point out that as is illustrated by the Amarna correspondence, that the city rulers served as the executive agents of Egypt in administering Canaan.

In simple terms, we know that God is immutable – he does not change. God states in Malachi 3:6, 'I the Lord do not change'. This is also attested to in James 1:17: 'Every good and perfect gift is from above, coming down from the Father of the heavenly lights, who does not change like shifting shadows'. Marcion's assertion that the God of the Old Testament and the God of the New Testament are different is thus refuted. If we now turn to another attribute of God, his holiness, we find this attested in Revelation 15:4, in the statement, 'For you alone are holy'. As Pink[42] states, 'Holiness is the very excellency of the Divine nature: the great God is "glorious in holiness" (Exodus 15:11)'. Because God is holy, he hates sin, which is contrary to his law. God's justice demands the punishment of sin. God's patience with the Israelites after the exodus, whilst they were

---

[42] Arthur W. Pink, *The Attributes of God* (Grand Rapids: Baker, 1975), p.51.

wandering in the desert (and subsequently) is well documented in Scripture. This deferral of justice illustrates the long-suffering and grace of God, but his patience cannot be taken for granted. God can act against sinners, and with justice, at any time. That he acted against the sinful Canaanites at a time of his choosing should not be a surprise to us (unless perhaps we are surprised that he did not act earlier).

Jesus' teaching that we should love our enemies is not found in the Old Testament. We can see here the New Covenant love principle, predicated on the love of God, exhibited in the sending of his Son and his redemptive work on the cross at Calvary and subsequent resurrection. God has not changed, but now he has provided gracious provision for the sinner who repents. Circumstances have indeed changed, and we can rejoice in the divine providence of almighty God.

Chapter Five
WARFARE

Introduction

The title of this chapter is admittedly a little misleading. The five episodes outlined here do not necessarily occur in the context of outright set-piece military action with opposing armies attacking and inflicting the highest possible numbers of deaths and casualties on their opponents, as is common in war. Rather, we are looking at particular individual episodes of causing the death of another which occurred in the context of conflict, either potential or actual. They each exhibit individual and distinctive motives for effecting death (except perhaps in the case of Jael, where her motivation for her murderous actions is arguably more obscure).

In modern warfare there are recognised rules to be respected. These are enshrined in the Geneva Convention. Although this nomenclature is widely known, its contents are much less so. Given this, it is worth briefly reviewing it, as it provides a useful yardstick for comparison with the norms of earlier (including ancient) warfare.

At the time of writing, the Geneva Convention is topical. Russia recently invaded Ukraine, to international opprobrium, and Amnesty International has just announced that prisoners of war from this conflict must have their rights respected under the Third Geneva Convention (which includes provisions for their treatment). There are already multiple assertions in the media claiming contravention of international accords by Russian troops.

The Geneva Conventions were signed in 1949 following the Second World War, and were intended to limit the horrors of war to humanity. Essentially they are based on the following principles:

- Hospitals and their staff in warzones must be free to operate safely
- Battle casualties are entitled to appropriate treatment
- Prisoners of war must be treated humanely
- Civilians and civilian infrastructure (such as power and water supplies) must be protected.

In 1977 two protocols were added to the 1949 Conventions. These provisions included the banning of the following:

- Taking hostages
- Terrorism
- Pillage
- Slavery
- Group punishment
- Humiliating or degrading treatment

It is unnecessary to examine these in detail. The headings are sufficient to provide a basic understanding of what is entailed. It should be carefully noted that the Geneva Conventions only relate to prisoners of war and non-combatants. This is not always appreciated.

Another major concern in modern conflict is the nature of the weapons used. This is an area of great importance with the development of biological and chemical weapons which are a relatively recent development. Conventional weapons are dealt with in the Hague Conventions of 1899 and 1907, and the Geneva Protocol addresses the use of biological and chemical weapons.

Ancient warfare was not bound by any international agreements. On the other hand, neither did they possess weapons of mass destruction that are available today. Battles in ancient times were very bloody affairs, with horrific injuries, and very limited medical treatments available. Civilians, including women and children, were not afforded any special dispensation, and were often killed indiscriminately or sold into slavery. No one had any special 'rights'.

We now come to the characters featured in this chapter, Ehud, Jael, Abner, Phinehas, and David. Five killings; five killers, all in the context of conflict, but all with differing motivation. These incidents will bc examined in more detail in the pages which follow.

PHINEHAS

Numbers 25:1-8

> While Israel was staying in Shittim, the men began to indulge in sexual immorality with Moabite women, who invited them to the sacrifices to their gods. The people ate the sacrificial meal and bowed down before these gods. So Israel yoked themselves to the Baal of Peor. And the Lord's anger burned against them.
>
> The Lord said to Moses, 'Take all the leaders of these people, kill them and expose them in broad daylight before the Lord, so that the Lord's fierce anger may turn away from Israel.'
>
> So Moses said to Israel's judges, 'Each of you must put to death those of your people who have yoked themselves to the Baal of Peor.'
>
> Then an Israelite man brought into the camp a Midianite woman right before the eyes of Moses and the whole assembly of Israel while they were weeping at the entrance to the tent of meeting. When Phinehas son of Eleazer, the son of Aaron, the priest, saw this, he left the assembly, took a spear in his hand and followed the Israelite into the tent. He drove the spear into both of them, right through the Israelite man and into the woman's stomach. Then the plague against the Israelites was stopped; but those who died in the plague numbered 24,000.

In today's world one can easily imagine the lurid headlines in the red-top tabloids in reporting this incident. Two people impaled whilst making love! We cannot, as is so often the case, project back into history the values of our own culture and judge accordingly.

The nation of Israel at this point are still traipsing around in the desert. After leaving Egypt in the exodus, their journey to the promised land, which should have been relatively brief, has been extended to forty years because of their lapse into unfaithfulness. God's good providence in effecting their redemption from slavery was soon forgotten, and their faith in him, which should have been unswerving, was easily derailed. Indeed, as Olson[43] remarks, the narrative in Numbers 25 'displays the fickle faith and shallow commitment of the old generation'. By 'old generation', the author is referring to the original cohort of Israelites who left Egypt, were unfaithful, and as a result were subsequently barred from entry into the promised land (with the exceptions of Joshua and Caleb). The account here follows on immediately after the appearance of Balaam in Numbers 22-24. He had been instructed by Balak, king of Moab, to curse the Israelites, but he failed to do so, and Balak was prevented from military victory over Israel.

Nonetheless, freedom from potential conflict did not result in Israel turning toward God in grateful thanks and worship for his gracious providence. Rather, they did the opposite as can be seen from the beginning of the passage quoted above. They engaged in illicit sexual relations with the Moabite women and were hence drawn into the worship practices of their gods. One might make some comparison here with the apostasy which took place at the time of the golden calf incident in Exodus 32, which occurred not long after the exit from Egypt.

God instructs Moses to kill the leaders of this rebellion against his precepts, and he in turn passes on the command to the judges of Israel. It is at this point that an Israelite male blatantly parades a Moabite woman before Moses and other Israelites who are mourning the developments at the entrance to the tent of meeting. Here one can appreciate the stark contrast between a group of worshippers of God, weeping at the apostasy of the people, and the insouciance of the Israelite man and his Moabite innamorata waltzing by on their way to have sex.

Phinehas is zealous for God and heedful of his instruction to Moses. He grabs a spear and without delay follows the pair into the tent and

[43] Dennis T. Olson, *Numbers*, IBC (Louisville: John Knox, 1996), p.152.

drives it through both of them with fatal results. The obvious implication from the text is that at the time of their death, the pair were having sexual relations.

With this act the plague stops, but not before 24,000 have lost their lives.

Notably, this is the first time we read of the pagan god Baal in the Hebrew Bible. Sadly, he would feature prominently in the history of Israel in the years to come.

It is appropriate here to provide further details of the hero of the story, as his significance to the history of Israel does not end here. First, it should be noted that he was the son of Eleazer, the son of Aaron (the High Priest), and thus of impressive lineage. Following the episode under consideration here, in verses 10-13, we learn that he was rewarded by God, not only with praise, but also that the priesthood would remain in his family in perpetuity. Yet this is not the last we read of him in the biblical record. God commanded vengeance on the Midianites, and in the resultant battle, in which the Israelites were victorious, Phinehas accompanied the troops (Numbers 31:6). In Joshua 22:13-32 we learn that he headed the delegation from Shiloh to protest at the altar which had been erected by the trans-Jordan tribes of Israel. Happily this dispute ended peacefully. Notably, his actions on the day we are considering here feature in the Psalms:

> But Phineas stood up and intervened, and the plague was checked. This was credited to him as righteousness for endless generations to come. (Psalm 106:30-31)

In today's world, Phinehas' act would indubitably be thought to constitute a criminal offence. However, as we so often have to remember, Israel is a theocracy. It is God who makes the law and not humans. God is their supreme authority, just as he is for Christians today. God decreed that the Israelites worship him and him only in the Decalogue, the Ten Commandments, documented in Exodus 20 and Deuteronomy 5. Idolatry was a heinous offence against God, punishable only by death (Deuteronomy 17:2-7). We, today, should remember that idolatry does not end with physical representations of so-called gods such as we read about in Isaiah 44 and Jeremiah 10. As Spender[44] has noted,

> The Bible understands that idolatry extends beyond the worship of images and false gods. It is a matter of the heart, associated with pride, self-centredness, greed, gluttony (Philippians 3:15), and a love for possessions (Matthew 6:24).

EHUD

Judges 3:15-30

> Again the Israelites cried out to the Lord, and he gave them a deliverer – Ehud, a left-handed man, the son of Gera the Benjaminite. The Israelites sent him with tribute to Eglon king of Moab.
>
> Now Ehud had made a double-edged sword about a cubit long, which he strapped to his right thigh under his clothing. He presented the tribute to Eglon king of Moab, who was a very fat man. After Ehud had presented the tribute, he sent on their way those who had carried it. But on reaching the stone images near Gilgal he himself went back to Eglon and said, 'Your majesty, I have a secret message for you.'
>
> The king said to his attendants, 'Leave us!' And they all left.
>
> Ehud then approached him while he was sitting alone in the upper room of his palace and said, 'I have a message from God for you.' As the king rose from his seat, Ehud reached with his left hand, drew the sword from his right thigh and plunged it into the king's belly. Even the handle sank in after the blade, and his bowels discharged. Ehud did not pull the sword out, and the fat closed in over it. Then Ehud went out to the porch; he

---

[44] Robert D. Spender, in *Evangelical Dictionary of Theology* (Grand Rapids: Zondervan, 1996), p.365.

> shut the doors of the upper room behind him and locked them.
>
> After he had gone, the servants came and found the doors of the upper room locked. They said, He must be relieving himself in the inner room of the palace.' They waited to the point of embarrassment, but when he did not open the doors of the room, they took a key and unlocked them. There they saw their lord fallen to the floor, dead.
>
> While they waited, Ehud got away. He passed by the stone images and escaped to Seirah. When he arrived there, he blew a trumpet in the hill country of Ephraim, and the Israelites went down with him from the hills, with him leading them.
>
> 'Follow me,' he ordered, 'for the Lord has given Moab, your enemy, into your hands.' So they followed him down and took possession of the fords of the Jordan that led to Moab; they allowed no one to cross over. At that time they struck down about ten thousand Moabites, all vigorous and strong; not one escaped. That day Moab was made subject to Israel, and the land had peace for eighty years.

We are in the period of the judges. This is the period between the conquest of Canaan and the advent of the monarchy in 1 Samuel. It is an unsettled period characterised by cycles of disobedience by Israel to God's precepts, followed by divine judgement on them by way of them being oppressed, and then a deliverer being raised up by God leading to liberation. The last verse of the book (21:25) summarises well when it says, 'In those days Israel had no king; everyone did as they saw fit'. Unfortunately the nation was slow to learn, and this cycle of events is repeated six times in the Book of Judges. Ehud is one such deliverer, and appears early in the book.

The precursor to the Ehud incident is found in Judges 3:12-14. The Israelites have fallen into sin, God gives Eglon, king of Moab, power over them. They cry for divine aid, and God then sends a deliverer,

Ehud, to rescue them from their plight. The cyclical nature of events described above is clearly illustrated here.

The Israelites send Ehud and a team of men to transport tribute to King Eglon. This probably means a set amount of goods demanded by him. The Israelites were in subservience to Eglon at the time, and not in a position to refuse any of his demands. Notably, Ehud is reported to be left-handed (Block[45] suggests he was ambidextrous). Before setting out on his journey he fashions a dagger-type weapon around 18 inches long which he secretes on his right thigh under his clothing. Being here, rather than on the left would have been an unusual site to carry a weapon, and thus would render it less likely to detection.

Ehud and his colleagues deliver the tribute to Eglon and, mission accomplished, they leave to return home. However, having travelled a limited distance, Ehud returns to the palace, claiming to have a secret message for the king. In order to maintain confidentiality, the king dismisses his attendants, and he sees Ehud in private in the upper room of the palace. Ehud now tells the king that he has a divine message for him, the king starts to get up, and Ehud draws his weapon and stabs the king in his abdomen. Such is the king's obesity that the weapon is virtually or completely submerged in the layers of fat, and he is faecally incontinent. Ehud locks the door to the room and makes good his escape. When the servants found the door locked, they assumed Eglon was relieving himself, and likely they smelled the odour of excrement which would have both confirmed their suspicion and reassured them as to his well-being. When an inordinate amount of time had passed with no evidence of the king's person, they did unlock the door, and found Eglon's body.

By this time, Ehud had had the time to make his escape. When he arrived at Seirah he blew a trumpet, summoned the Israelite troops, led them to a stunning victory over the forces of Moab, and verse 30 tells us: 'That day Moab was made subject to Israel, and the land had peace for eighty years'.

Ehud was an assassin. He, with subterfuge and consummate skill, killed king Eglon. It is the sort of plot that one might expect from a

---

[45] Daniel I. Block, *Judges, Ruth*, NAC (Nashville: B&H, 1999), p.160-161.

modern-day thriller, albeit transported in time. It is also not devoid of humour, admittedly black humour.

That the outcome for Israel is tremendous cannot be denied. Their eighteen-year subjugation to Moab is at an end, Moab is now under Israelite control, and there is going to be peace for the next eighty years. That is, until the Israelite nation once more sinks into apostasy and needs another deliverer, this time the prophet Deborah.

Ehud committed a deliberate and calculated act in ending Eglon's life. By the terms of modern legislation, this undoubtedly constitutes an act of murder. Israel was not technically at war with Moab at the material time, so any argument that this killing took place in the context of formal hostilities between the two nations is not credible (nevertheless this incident is included in the 'warfare' section of this book, given the hostility between Moab and the Israelites, and the fact that armed struggle commenced immediately afterwards).

Christians may find themselves in something of a dilemma here. There is, on the one hand, the carefully planned brutal killing of a king, and yet a few verses later the perpetrator is leading the Israelite army against the Moabite forces, ordering them to follow him because God has given them into their hands. Commentators have debated this point and come to different conclusions. A reasonable conclusion is drawn by Lawson Younger[46] who writes:

> Accordingly, it is possible – and perhaps preferable – to see the Ehud story operating on both the human and divine levels. Thus, Ehud is undoubtedly not an Othniel. He depends on his own crafty, stealthy, deceptive plot to assassinate Eglon. He is treacherous and brutal. His characterization is an important element in the larger context of the book. Yet God uses him in spite of his flaws in order to emphasize his mercy and compassion on his people (even though they are not serving him and have not repented). Moreover, God manifests his justice in judging wickedness and oppression as evidenced in Eglon and the Moabites.

---

[46] K. Lawson Younger Jr., *Judges/Ruth*, NIVAC (Grand Rapids: Zondervan, 2002), p.124.

JAEL

Judges 4:16-22

Barak pursued the chariots and army as far as Harosheth Haggoyim, and all Sisera's troops fell by the sword; not a man was left. Sisera, meanwhile, fled on foot to the tent of Jael, the wife of Heber the Kenite, because there was an alliance between Jabin king of Hazor and the family of Heber the Kenite.

Jael went out to meet Sisera and said to him, 'Come, my lord, come right in. Don't be afraid.' So he entered her tent, and she covered him with a blanket.

'I'm thirsty,' he said. 'Please give me some water.' She opened a skin of milk, gave him a drink, and covered him up.

'Stand in the doorway of the tent,' he told her. 'If someone comes and asks you, "Is anyone in there?" say "No."'

But Jael, Heber's wife, picked up a tent peg and a hammer and went quietly to him while he lay fast asleep, exhausted. She drove the peg through his temple into the ground, and he died.

Just then Barak came by in pursuit of Sisera, and Jael went out to meet him. 'Come,' she said, 'I will show you the man you're looking for.' So he went in with her, and there lay Sisera with the tent peg through his temple – dead.

Judges 5:24-27

In this passage from the Song of Deborah, Jael's actions are commemorated.

At this time, Jabin, king of the Canaanites, had been oppressing the Israelites. He had a huge army of chariots, and the battle power of this force should not be underestimated. Indeed, McMath[47] compares it to a modern aircraft-carrier battle group. Significantly, he also notes that the chariot soldiers would have had to be full time professional soldiers in order to properly train and prepare for their combat role. Given that those men fielded by the Israelites would have been at least in a very large part farmers who would only take up arms on an occasional basis, and by contrast be relatively untrained, the forces here, on the face of it, would have been decidedly mismatched, and an impartial observer would not be likely to put his money on the Israelites being victorious in any formal conflict.

Deborah was serving at that time as a prophetess in Israel. This was a very unusual state of affairs, but in brief, she galvanised Barak and the Israelites to do battle with Jabin's forces who were under the command of General Sisera. Hostilities commenced, and contrary to logical expectation, Sisera's troops were routed. Cundall and Morris[48] postulate that there was a storm before the battle, that the Israelites attacked from the high ground, and that the now softened ground in the valley greatly impeded the manoeuvrability of the enemy chariots. As the chariot force retreated back towards their base camp the valley narrowed, and the resulting traffic congestion would have further added to the Canaanites' difficulties. Given the likely chaotic vehicular congestion, Sisera, their commander, effects his escape on foot.

Enter Jael. Her husband, Heber the Kenite, has already been introduced in Judges 4:11, clearly to contextualise what is to follow. The Kenites were nomads but did have some association with the tribe of Judah. Nevertheless, they had a peace agreement with King Jabin. Thus, when Sisera in his flight comes to the tent of Heber and Jael (Heber is evidently not there), he would have had no cause to be concerned for his safety. Indeed, given the then conventions of hospitality, he is likely to have felt assured that he had indeed arrived at a safe shelter.

---

[47] John McMath, in *The Moody Bible Commentary*, ed. Michael Rydelnik and Michael Vanlaningham (Chicago: Moody, 2014), p.367.
[48] Arthur E. Cundall and Leon Morris, *Judges & Ruth*, TOTC (Downers Grove: IVP, 1968), p.87-88.

Jael goes out of the tent to meet Sisera, and invites him in, while at the same time telling him not to be afraid. She is thus both welcoming and reassuring. Inside the tent, she provides a blanket and feeds him buttermilk. He asks her to tell any enquirers that there is no one else in the tent, and exhausted, he goes to sleep.

With Sisera asleep and thus unsuspecting and incapacitated, Jael takes a tent peg and a hammer, and drives the peg through Sisera's head, pinning his body to the ground.

Barak, Deborah's general then arrives in pursuit of Sisera, and Jael shows him the corpse.

Deborah understandably celebrates Jael's actions in Judges 5:24. This is understandable on the basis that killing an enemy of Israel makes you a friend of Israel.

Whereas, as Christians, our inclinations and sympathies are with Israel, is it not appropriate to consider this event in more dispassionate terms? Is this not an act of brutal murder?

First, it cannot be argued that it was not an unlawful killing because it was an act of war. The Canaanites were certainly at war with Israel, but Judges 4:17 tells us that 'there was an alliance between Jabin king of Hazor and the family of Heber the Kenite'.

Second, not only does she kill Sisera, Jael lulls him into a false sense of security by her friendly greeting and hospitable actions. She then, in a premeditated way, whilst he is defenceless, kills him in a brutal manner. When Barak subsequently arrives, there is no hint of remorse for her actions. Indeed, it is possible to infer that she gives the impression of being proud of her actions.

Yes, at least in modern legal terms, this is murder! It would be very difficult, I think, to persuade a jury otherwise. Yet this is a Bible story. We tell it to our children in Sunday School without any sense of criticism of Jael. How can this be? In terms of the conventions of ANE (Ancient Near Eastern) hospitality, which were very strong, (as is clear from elsewhere in the Old Testament), this was a heinous deed.

A forensic psychiatrist instructed to prepare a court report today for either defence or prosecution would doubtless be seeking the motivation behind her lethal behaviour. For me, this is the most enigmatic facet of what in many ways must be considered a very unusual case of homicide.

Jael's motivation for her homicidal actions is not clear from the biblical text. The comment of Block[49] is arguably an apt conclusion here:

> However, just because the author records her deeds does not mean he approves of them. It simply adds to the mystery of divine providence, demonstrating implicitly what the following verses explicitly affirm: God is able to incorporate the free activities of human beings into his plan for his own glory and for the salvation of his people.

ABNER

2 Samuel 2:17-23

> The battle that day was very fierce, and Abner and the Israelites were defeated by David's men.
>
> The three sons of Zeruiah were there: Joab, Abishai and Asahel. Now Asahel was as fleet-footed as a wild gazelle. He chased Abner, turning neither to the right nor to the left as he pursued him. Abner looked behind him and asked, 'Is that you, Asahel?'
>
> 'It is,' he answered.
>
> Then Abner said to him, 'Turn aside to the right or to the left; take on one of the young men and strip him of his weapons.' But Asahel would not stop chasing him.
>
> Again Abner warned Asahel, 'Stop chasing me! Why should I strike you down? How could I look your brother Joab in the face?'

---

[49] Daniel I. Block, *Judges, Ruth*, NAC (Nashville: B&H, 1999), p.210.

> But Asahel refused to give up the pursuit; so Abner thrust the butt of his spear into Asahel's stomach, and the spear came out through his back. He fell there and died on the spot. And every man stopped when he came to the place where Asahel had fallen and died.

At this time in Israel's history, the kingdom is divided. David has been anointed king over Judah in the south of the country and has settled in Hebron. Saul is now dead (1 Samuel 31). With his decease, Abner, the commander of Saul's army (1 Samuel 14:50), appears to have been the person to step into the power vacuum. He installed one of Saul's sons, Ish-Bosheth, as king. Ish-Bosheth presumably did not engage in the battle of Gilboa in which Saul lost his life (1 Samuel 31).

A civil war began between David's forces and those of Abner/Ish-Bosheth. In a decisive battle, David was successful in beating the opposition. As can be learned from the biblical passage at the beginning of this chapter, Abner flees, pursued by Asahel. Asahel, Joab, and Abishai were the sons of David's sister Zeruiah, and Joab was the commander of David's forces.

Abner, seeing the sprinting Asahel chasing him, tries to persuade him to chase someone he could be more evenly matched with in a fight (vv.20-21). Abner was clearly militarily very skilled. He had recognised his pursuer and did not want enmity between himself and Joab, with the inevitable consequences if he killed Joab's brother. Asahel did not listen. He is run through with the butt of Abner's spear and dies.

There is no doubt that Abner's actions have resulted in the death of Asahel. The text states that 'Abner thrust the butt of his spear into Asahel's stomach' (v.23), but on the other hand it is the butt of his spear, not the offensive end of his weapon which was used. It has been suggested that while Abner was running away, he suddenly stopped, Asahel was unable to check himself in time, and ran into the spear.

Some will doubtless wonder how running into the back of the spear could have resulted in such a grave penetrating wound. In Roman times, legionary soldiers were armed with a sword (gladius) and usually two throwing spears (pila). Although only the offensive end of the pilum was metal tipped, there was normally a point to the base of the spear. This meant that the soldier could, when at rest, stick it upright in the ground. It seems reasonable to wonder whether a similar arrangement existed in respect of Abner's spear, and that its base was not blunt, but sharpened for a similar purpose.

It is not uncommon, when examining those accused of causing death by stabbing, to be told that 'he just ran on to the knife'. Such can be the ease of entry of a sharp knife into soft tissue that such an impression might be given. Nonetheless, the biblical text does inform that Abner 'thrust', implying a deliberate and purposeful act.

In today's world, if these events took place outside of the theatre of war, Abner would almost certainly be charged with the offence of murder. Unless the charge was altered by the prosecution pre-trial, the defence would almost certainly enter a plea of not guilty to murder but guilty to manslaughter, perhaps on the basis of lack of intent to murder, although any such plea would be largely dependent on the physical characteristics of the spear: was its base sharpened or not? Much would also be made of the way in which Abner had tried to persuade Asahel to desist from his pursuit, and it would be suggested that despite the 'thrust' content of the evidence, that Asahel had by his own momentum run onto the 'blunt' end of the spear, and had thereby contributed to his own death in no small way.

As already noted, jury decisions are not always easy to predict. Nevertheless, in this case I think it not unlikely that the arguments of the defence would prevail. Abner might well be convicted of manslaughter rather than murder.

Knife crime is common these days, and the story of Abner and Asahel is a salutary reminder of how sharp weapons can have fatal consequences, even if death is not the intended result.

This story is also a reminder of how one offence can lead to further offending. Joab was incensed by the death of his brother. He sought revenge, and how he went about this will occupy a later portion of this book.

DAVID

1 Samuel 17:38-51

Then Saul dressed David in his own tunic. He put a coat of armour on him and a bronze helmet on his head. David fastened on his sword over the tunic and tried walking around, because he was not used to them.

'I cannot go in these,' he said to Saul, 'because I am not used to them.' So he took them off. Then he took his staff in his hand, chose five smooth stones from the stream, put them in the pouch of his shepherd's bag and, with his sling in his hand, approached the Philistine.

Meanwhile, the Philistine, with his shield-bearer in front of him, kept coming closer to David. He looked David over and saw that he was little more than a boy, glowing with health and handsome, and he despised him. He said to David, 'Am I a dog that you come at me with sticks?' And the Philistine cursed David by his gods. 'Come here,' he said, 'and I'll give your flesh to the birds and the wild animals!'

David said to the Philistine, 'You come against me with sword and spear and javelin, but I come against you in the name of the Lord Almighty, the God of the armies of Israel, whom you have defied. This day the Lord will deliver you into my hands, and I'll strike you down and cut off your head This very day I will give the carcasses of the Philistine army to the birds and the wild animals, and the whole world will know that there is a God in Israel. All those gathered here will know that it is not by sword or spear that the Lord saves; for the battle is the Lord's, and he will give all of you into our hands.'

As the Philistine moved closer to attack him, David ran quickly towards the battle line to meet him. Reaching into his bag and taking out a stone, he slung it and struck the Philistine on the forehead. The stone sank into his forehead, and he fell face down on the ground.

> So David triumphed over the Philistine with a sling and a stone; without a sword in his hand he struck down the Philistine and killed him.
>
> David ran and stood over him. He took hold of the Philistine's sword and drew it from the sheath. After he killed him, he cut off his head with the sword.

Too many Christians fail to translate this story, popular in Sunday School, into an adult appreciation in their later years. Their thinking often does not progress beyond the picture of a boy picking up pebbles and waving a piece of cloth around the size of a tea towel, in the face of a huge, armoured man of fearsome appearance, found in books of Bible stories for children. Such may be suitable for children but is essentially divorced from the reality of what happened.

The antecedents to this spectacle are that the Israelite and Philistine armies are facing each other with a view to battle. Sometimes in those days there would be a fight between the champions of each army, and the outcome would decide the winner between the two sides. This benefitted both parties in the sense that only one individual would be killed, as opposed to multiple deaths on both sides.

Some might think that King Saul should have fought as Israel's champion. There is much to support such a contention. He was king, and led the Israelite army. Indeed, one might infer this from the people's response to Samuel, when he warned them against their desire for a monarch, in 1 Samuel 8: 19-20:

> But the people refused to listen to Samuel. 'No!' they said. 'We want a king over us. Then we shall be like all the other nations, with a king to lead us and go out before us and fight our battles.

Although shorter than Goliath, Saul was 'a head taller than anyone else' (1 Samuel 9:2). He also had bronze armour (1 Samuel 17:38-39), and few if any of his soldiers would have been similarly equipped. The one thing he was lacking was courage. Verse 24 informs that when Goliath would shout his challenges that 'Whenever the Israelites saw the man, they all fled from him in great fear'. This would have included King Saul. Saul is clearly in a difficult position here. He, the obvious person to act as Israel's champion, is too afraid to step up to the mark. He makes what would ordinarily be an almost irresistible offer to his troops: Kill Goliath and you will be wealthy, have the hand of my daughter, and your family will never have to pay any taxes (v.25). Still no takers! Goliath looks unassailable.

Enter David. He eschews the offer of Saul's armour. He was unused to it, and it would have severely impeded his freedom of movement. He takes five smooth stones and approaches Goliath with his sling. Goliath, with his usual loud bravado, belittles David. Goliath is heavily armoured and strongly weaponed. David responds to his murderous threats by telling him that he comes in the name of the Lord Almighty. As Goliath moves forward, David does the same, and slings a stone, striking Goliath on the forehead. Goliath is floored, and David cuts off his head with his own sword.

It should be noted that the circumstances here are very different from the way in which we often imagine, particularly in terms of how we often think of David's sling. First, the smooth stones that David picked up would not have been the little pebbles often imagined. Second, his sling would not have been the simple piece of cloth we sometimes see him pictured waving in books of Bible stories for children. This was a pouch with cords at each end. It would be whirled (probably) on a vertical axis rather than round and round over the head, and one end released to send the stone on its way. Although used by shepherds, it was also a military weapon, and one which could be used with astonishing accuracy by those practiced in its use. Indeed, Judges tells us of the Benjaminites: 'Among all these soldiers there were seven hundred select troops who were left-handed, each of whom could sling a stone at a hair and not miss.' (Judges 20:16). Additionally, the stones employed were not small pebbles as is often imagined today. They were often the size of tennis balls, and when discharged from the whirling sling could travel at speeds of over 100 miles an hour. No wonder that the bones of Goliath's forehead were crushed at the impact! David was not as punily armed as is often thought.

David killed Goliath, but in the context of war between the two opposing sides. There was an agreed contest between the champions of both sides. David, and hence Israel, won the battle.

No offence was committed.

As a postscript here, it is noted that the story of David and Goliath is often used metaphor for standing up to the 'Goliaths', using the term Goliath as a metaphor for difficult or challenging situations in our lives. We on our own are but weak and ineffective, but with God's assistance can successfully face up to the Goliaths in the context of our own existence etcetera. I personally find this an inapt analogy, albeit conceding it may have its uses in the Sunday School. I think it likely that what the writer of this historical document is seeking to convey (as elsewhere in this book) is the contrast between the characterological features of David and Saul, and by that, their relative suitability for the Israelite throne.

Discussion

These five incidents, albeit occurring in the context of war, or at least of conflict, potential or otherwise, are very different in many ways. They illustrate that the act of killing, although all such incidents have elements in common, does vary widely in its circumstances. We might think, amongst other factors, of the characters of the perpetrators, the degree of planning (or otherwise), the method used, the motivation, and their mental state at the time of the killing. Obviously, the latter in particular is of more than passing interest to me as a forensic psychiatrist.

Turning first to their characters, it is important to note that the descriptive elements in the Bible are there for theological reasons, and not for the purpose of psychiatric dissection! Some possibilities, even likelihoods, for personality traits can be inferred, but the Bible as a whole does not provide sufficient information to classify (probably) any of its host of characters into any of the many categories of personality disorder in the two main current psychiatric classificatory systems. Nevertheless, we might well think of Ehud as being a man capable of shrewd and detailed planning, a logical thinker who knows what he is doing, and the end point he is seeking to achieve. Phinehas was zealous for the honour of the Lord (Numbers 25:10). Jael is something of a mystery. Yet she commits an act one would not usually associate with the female gender. She must have had strong internal resources (and a strong stomach) to act as she did. Whatever her motive, she was a strong and determined woman, and willing to commit a heinous act to achieve her goal. Abner clearly did not want to kill Asahel, if for no other reason that he did not want to antagonise and gain the enmity of his brother Joab, who one might suspect to be something of a fearsome character in his own right. David was also zealous for God's honour and had every confidence in the power of the living God for a successful outcome in his encounter with Goliath (1 Samuel 17:36-37).

Ehud pre-planned his assassination as has already been noted. Phinehas acted on the spur of the moment, reacting to the immediate circumstances as they presented, and in accordance with divine command. Abner also reacted to his particular situation, albeit reluctantly, and possibly without intending the outcome. We cannot suppose that Jael could have predicted that General Sisera would turn up on her doorstep, neither that the Israelite army would have comprehensively defeated his very formidable forces. We must therefore assume that she reacted to the circumstances as they presented themselves.

All the victims' deaths were probably from penetrating wounds. Ehud used a sword concealed for that specific purpose, Phinehas used a spear, presumably one handily available, and Abner used the spear that he had taken into battle. Jael made use of household implements that would have been the possession of all tent-dwellers. David's sling stone crushed Goliath's frontal bone, without necessarily being immediately fatal, but the subsequent decapitation would indubitably have been so.

The motivation in each case has already been examined, and is clear, other than in the case of Jael.

So far as their mental state at the time of the killings is concerned, this is difficult to ascertain given the scanty information available. We can be confident that Ehud was acting in clear consciousness, and with full knowledge of what he was doing. Phinehas likewise. With Jael the position is less clear, but she behaved in an unremarkable way towards Sisera when he appeared at her tent, and her actions in terms of terminating his life, whilst arguably gruesome, were performed in logical and deadly sequence. Abner, whilst probably reluctant to slay Asahel, wanted to preserve his own life, and was acutely aware that Joab, arguably a much greater threat to him, was on his trail, together with his brother Abishai. He would have been in a desperate frame of mind. I would note here that none of this, at least on the face of it, (with the possible exception of Abner), would constitute a defence to a charge of murder in today's U.K.

Chapter Six

REGICIDE

Introduction

Decades ago, when I was studying for O level English Literature, the required Shakespeare play for the examination was Macbeth. William Shakespeare wrote this play in 1606, and it was intended to reinforce the idea, current at that time, of the Divine Right of Kings. Briefly, this concept asserts that the king's right to rule derives from divine authority, and thus they are not subject to the direction of any earthly authority such as the people, the aristocracy, or even a parliament. It follows from that basic premise that any attempt to remove them (which, obviously, would include killing them), would be contrary to the will of God and hence be sacrilege.

Regicide is the killing of a monarch and is often enacted in the course of an attempt by another or others for the purposes of seizing power. One can see a plethora of such events over the course of history. In the UK we probably think first of King Charles I. He was a strong adherent of the concept of the divine right of kings as mentioned above. He made his adherence to this belief clear even after the first English civil war, when he was imprisoned by the Parliamentarians. They soon concluded that they could not negotiate meaningfully with him, and neither did they trust him not to pursue further military action against them. They reluctantly concluded that the only solution was to execute him, and he was beheaded on 30th January 1649.

As Christians, we are interested in the first century AD, the time when Jesus lived, the early church was formed, and the New Testament was written. At that time the Roman Empire ruled the then-known world. There were twelve Roman Emperors during that time. Of these, Gaius (commonly known as Caligula), Galba, Otho, Vitellius, and Domitian, were assassinated (although some may prefer to think that Vitellius was executed). There are also strong suggestions that Claudius was fatally poisoned by his wife Agrippina, and suspicion that Titus was poisoned by his younger brother Domitian.

Monarchies are largely redundant in today's world other than for ceremonial purposes, although the Royal Family continues to engender much affection in the hearts of the British public. Nevertheless, the concept of regicide continues with the execution of heads of state, and most will immediately think of the assassination of President Kennedy in Dallas in 1963. There are many more examples, some better known than others. Below is a list of heads of state assassinated after the death of President Kennedy:

- 1966. Hendrik Verwoerd, Prime Minister of South Africa
- 1975. Faisal, King of Saudi Arabia
- 1975. Mujibur Rahman, President of Bangladesh
- 1979. Park Chung Lee, President of South Korea
- 1981. Ziaur Rahman, President of Bangladesh
- 1981. Mohammed Ali Rajai and Hojjatoleslam Mohammed Javad Bahonar, President and Prime Minister of Iran respectively
- 1981. Anwar Sadat, President of Egypt
- 1982. Beshir Gemayel, President-elect of Lebanon
- 1983. Maurice Bishop, Prime Minister of Grenada
- 1984. Indira Gandhi, Prime Minister of India
- 1985. Olaf Palme, Prime Minister of Sweden
- 1995. Yitzak Rabin, Prime Minister of Israel
- 2001. Birendra, King of Nepal
- 2003. Zoran Dindic, Prime Minister of Serbia

It is therefore of no surprise that during the long period covered by the biblical record there are a number of killings of kings. It is equally predictable that the desire to gain power is a prominent feature. Here we will examine the roles of, Baasha, Zimri, Jehu, and Jehoiada, and their activities in ending the lives of rulers.

It is important to remember when considering the Old Testament Israelite kings that their role and responsibilities differed from those in other countries. In the rest of the world the king's word tended to be law and what he wanted he got. Worldly kings were autocrats. As The New Unger's Bible Dictionary[50] has it, the king of Israel was 'the viceroy of Jehovah'. 1 Timothy 1:17 describes God as the 'King eternal', and so he is. Israel was a theocracy, that is, it was ruled by God. Whilst, for example, David and Solomon were kings of Israel, they only held their positions because they were appointed by God. They had to obey his commands, and furthermore, had a responsibility to ensure that God's laws and commands were obeyed by their countrymen. They can be seen as conduits for the ultimate authority held by the Creator.

Even before Israel crossed the Jordan to enter the promised land it is clear that God had decreed that the nation would at some future stage be ruled by a king, for we find in the Book of Deuteronomy instructions for the monarchy, part of which is reproduced below and comes from Deuteronomy 17:18-20:

> When he takes the throne of his kingdom, he is to write for himself on a scroll a copy of this law, taken from that of the Levitical priests. It is to be with him, and he is to read it all the days of his life so that he may learn to revere the Lord his God and follow carefully all the words of this law and these decrees and not consider himself better than his fellow Israelites and turn from the law to the right or to the left. Then he and his descendants will reign a long time over his kingdom in Israel.

Old Testament history indicates that these strictures were largely ignored with predictable consequence.

---

[50] *The New Unger's Bible Dictionary*, ed. R. K. Harrison (Chicago: Moody, 1985), p.739.

AGAG

1 Samuel 15:1-9

> Samuel said to Saul, 'I am the one the Lord sent to anoint you king over his people Israel; so listen now to the message from the Lord. This is what the Lord Almighty says: 'I will punish the Amalekites for what they did to Israel when they waylaid then as they came up from Egypt. Now go, attack the Amalekites and totally destroy all that belongs to them. Do not spare them; put to death men and women, children and infants, cattle and sheep, camels and donkeys."'
>
> So Saul summoned the men and mustered them at Telaim – two hundred thousand foot soldiers and ten thousand from Judah. Saul went to the city of Amalek and set an ambush in the ravine. Then he said to the Kenites, 'Go away, leave the Amalekites so that I do not destroy you along with them; for you showed kindness to all the Israelites when they came up out of Egypt.' So the Kenites moved away from the Amalekites.
>
> Then Saul attacked the Amalekites all the way from Havilah to Shur, near the eastern border of Egypt. He took Agag king of the Amalekites alive, and all his people he totally destroyed with the sword. But Saul and the army spared Agag and the best of the sheep and cattle, the fat calves and lambs – everything that was good. These they were unwilling to destroy completely, but everything that was despised and weak they totally destroyed.

Here, the prophet Samuel relays to King Saul an instruction from God, specifically that he is to attack and 'totally destroy' the Amalekites. The verb for 'totally destroy' is the Hebrew word *herem*, which is used several times during this brief passage of Scripture. It is a very significant term in the context of this event, and as readers will recall, has already been discussed.

It is essential to recall the history the Israelites had with the Amalekites. They take their name from Amalek, who was a grandson of Esau (Genesis 36:12). The Amalekites are remembered for being the first people grouping to attack the Israelites at Rephidim after their emancipation from Egypt (Exodus 17:8-16), although their motivation is not specified. This encounter is often remembered as the time that whenever Moses held up his hands, Israel prevailed in the fighting, and the opposite occurred when he lowered them, leading to Aaron and Hur eventually supporting his hands. The Amalekites were overwhelmed by Israel on this occasion. God told Moses to write down an account of this battle, and issued the ominous words, 'I will completely blot out the name of Amalek from under heaven' (Exodus 17:14). Even after Israel entered the promised land, there was continued enmity from the Amalekites (Judges 3:12-14; 6:3-5, 33; 7:12). However, it is in the current portion of Scripture that Saul was to fulfil God's word in respect of the Amalekites and bring his judgement upon them.

The Kenites were a nomadic tribe who clearly lived among the Amalekites at the time of Saul's reign. In contrast to the Amalekites, the passage quoted above indicates that the Kenites 'showed kindness' to the Israelites following their exodus from Egypt, thus explaining Saul's warning to them, which they heeded.

As is clear, Saul's obedience to God's command is only partial. He spares Agag, the king of the Amalekites, and the best of the animals. Why the animals are spared is not the primary concern here, although one suspects his explanation is more than a trifle disingenuous. So far as his failure to execute King Agag is concerned, Evans[51] supplies a credible explanation: 'Probably Saul spared the king to display him as a trophy of war, which fits with his subsequent setting up a "monument in his own honor" in Carmel (1 Samuel 15:12)'. His flagrant flouting of a specific command of God was to incur a severe penalty: 'Because you have rejected the word of the Lord, he has rejected you as king' (1 Samuel 15:23b).

By verse 16 Samuel has had his fill of Saul's specious reasoning. 'Enough!' he cries. Saul's defence might fool the less discerning, but not the prophet of God. He sees through Saul's verbiage to the

---

[51] Paul S. Evans, *1-2 Samuel*, TSOGC (Grand Rapids: Zondervan, 2018), p.164.

motives at the heart of his actions. His riposte in verses 17-19 is one which a barrister might well admire! Saul is now very much on the back foot. Although insisting he did obey the divine instructions, it is noteworthy that in verse 21 he states: 'The soldiers took sheep and cattle from the plunder'. The psychiatrist in me would suggest that this is an example of a mental defence mechanism known as projection, where blame is transferred from oneself to another source. 'It wasn't me guv – it was him over there!' Saul may (and this is a very big may), have thought that using the animals as sacrifices to God fulfilled the divine command, but in a deferred manner. Such a suggestion is, I think, of limited credibility, but it is one raised by Evans.[52] Samuel's response merits reproduction in full (1 Samuel 15:22-23):

> Does the Lord delight in burnt offerings and sacrifices as much as obeying the Lord? To obey is better than sacrifice, and to heed is better than the fat of rams. For rebellion is like the sin of divination, and arrogance like the evil of idolatry. Because you have rejected the word of the Lord, he has rejected you as king.

God's judgement on Saul is announced!

Saul confesses his sin in that he has disobeyed the Lord's command. Yet even here, one has grounds for questioning his sincerity. Verse 24 states:

> Then Saul said to Samuel, 'I have sinned. I violated the Lord's command and your instructions. I was afraid of the men and so I gave in to them.

In his second sentence Saul is projecting some of the blame on to his men, just as he did before. He may be accepting *some* responsibility, but he is not accepting *all* responsibility. His repentance appears less than complete. In verse 31 we learn that 'Saul worshipped the Lord', but we remain uncertain as to the true state of his heart at that time.

After this emotionally charged dialogue, the denouement comes almost as an anti-climax. Samuel kills Agag.

---

[52] *Ibid*, p.166.

Saul, like other kings who were to follow, in both the northern and southern kingdoms, ignored the unique regnal arrangements of the Israelites: the supreme authority in government rested with God. Ultimate power was in the hands of the Almighty, not the king. The consequence of forgetting or ignoring this reality was catastrophic for Saul and would be so for other monarchs in the future.

It is pertinent to pause here for a moment and consider our own posture in respect of obedience to the precepts laid down by God. In particular, bearing in mind the common mental defence mechanism used by Saul, which probably most people employ many times daily, do we accept responsibility for our sinful acts, or do we try to project blame elsewhere?

BAASHA

1 Kings 15:25-30

> Nadab son of Jeroboam became king of Israel in the second year of Asa king of Judah, and he reigned over Israel for two years. He did evil in the eyes of the Lord, following the ways of his father and committing the same sin his father had caused Israel to commit.
>
> Baasha son of Ahijah from the tribe of Issachar plotted against him, and he struck him down at Gibbethon, a Philistine town, while Nadab and all Israel were besieging it. Baasha killed Nadab in the third year of Asa king of Judah and succeeded him as king.
>
> As soon as he began to reign, he killed Jeroboam's whole family. He did not leave Jeroboam anyone that breathed, but destroyed them all, according to the word of the Lord given through his servant Ahijah the Shilonite. This happened because of the sins Jeroboam had committed and had caused Israel to commit, and because he aroused the anger of the Lord, the God of Israel.

Once one gets past the reigns of Saul, David, and Solomon, and the country splits into north (Israel) and south (Judah), with kings in both realms, the regnal history becomes rather more complicated. After the death of King Solomon, his son and successor to the throne, Rehoboam, was asked if he would remove some of the taxes which his father had imposed. Instead of accepting the counsel of the older, and arguably wiser, of his advisors, he instead took the advice of his peers, who advocated their increase! The northern tribes revolted and made Jeroboam their king, and so the split occurred in 931/930 BC with the north subsequently being rather confusingly known as Israel, and the south as Judah (1 Kings 12:1-24).

There were nineteen kings in the north between the start and the end of the kingdom in 722 BC when the nation was defeated by the Assyrians, who deported the population, or at least most of them. As can be inferred, the average length of reign of the individual kings was relatively brief. All these kings are presented in the Bible as being bad. In contrast those in Judah were partly bad and partly good. In the north the kings came from nine different dynasties whereas in Judah, all were descended from David.

As noted in the passage above, Nadab succeeded his father, Jeroboam I, and he is recorded as continuing in the same sinful habits his father had practiced. This principally may be taken to refer to Jeroboam's apostate practices. When he came to power, in the context of the land being separated into north and south, he did not want those he ruled to travel to the temple in Jerusalem (God's chosen place, located in Judah), to worship. Instead, he instituted new worship practices. He built temples in Dan and Bethel with golden calves to represent the presence of God (1 Kings 12:25-33). One might recall here the golden calf that Aaron formed in Exodus 32, and its consequences. Jeroboam ignored the prophetic warnings he received, as documented in 1 Kings 13:1-14:20. This was to set a pattern for all the following kings in the northern kingdom.

As also recorded above, Baasha assassinated King Nadab during the siege of the city of Gibbethon. He did not stop there, but as was not uncommon for the time, killed Jeroboam's whole family, as had been predicted by the prophet Ahijah. The same fate was to be the case for his own family (1 Kings 16:11). It will readily be appreciated that the execution of a former king's relatives, particularly the male kin, reduced the chances of future claims to the throne, with all the potential conflict that might bring.

It is worth recalling here that there was enmity between Israel and Judah at the time of Baasha's reign. Asa was on the throne of Judah at the time, and relations between them were hostile.

Baasha reigned for 24 years, and apparently died a natural death. He was succeeded by his son Elah, of whom more in the next chapter.

There is little necessity for further comment here. Matters are straightforward. Nadab was king, Baasha wanted to be king, so Baasha assassinated Nadab. It is worthy of emphasis that Baasha's killing of the house of Jeroboam I had been foreseen by a prophet of the Lord, and also that the same fate awaited his own relatives.

ZIMRI

1 Kings 16: 1-13

> Then the word of the Lord came to Jehu son of Anani concerning Baasha: 'I lifted you up from the dust and appointed you ruler over my people Israel, but you followed the ways of Jeroboam and caused my people Israel to sin and to arouse my anger by their sins. So I am about to wipe out Baasha and his house, and I will make your house like that of Jeroboam son of Nebat. Dogs will eat those belonging to Baasha who die in the city, and birds will feed on those who die in the country.'
>
> As for the other events of Baasha's reign, what he did and his achievements, are they not written in the book of the annals of the kings of Israel? Baasha rested with his ancestors and was buried in Tirzah. And Elah his son succeeded him as king.
>
> Moreover, the word of the Lord came through the prophet Jehu son of Hanani to Baasha and his house, because of all the evil he had done in the eyes of the Lord, arousing his anger by the things he did, becoming like the house of Jeroboam – and also because he destroyed it.

> In the twenty-sixth year of Asa king of Judah, Elah son of Baasha became king of Israel, and he reigned in Tirzah for two years.
>
> Zimri, one of his officials, who had command of half his chariots, plotted against him. Elah was in Tirzah at the time, getting drunk in the home of Arza, the palace administrator at Tirzah. Zimri came in, struck him down and killed him in the twenty-seventh year of Asa king of Judah. Then he succeeded him as king.
>
> As soon as he began to reign and was seated on the throne, he killed off Baasha's whole family. He did not spare a single male, whether relative or friend. So Zimri destroyed the whole family of Baasha, in accordance of the word of the Lord spoken against Baasha through the prophet Jehu – because of all the sins Baasha and his son Elah had committed and had caused Israel to commit, so that they aroused the anger of the Lord, the God of Israel, by their worthless idols.

The monarchy in the north began with Jeroboam (as already noted), then came Nadab, his son. He was wicked, as his father had been, and he ruled for only two years before being assassinated by Baasha (as noted in the previous chapter), during a siege of the Philistine city of Gibbethon (1 Kings 15:25-28). Baasha, who reigned for 24 years was no model king either, and Scripture tells us that 'He did evil in the eyes of the Lord' (1 Kings 15:34). As the passage above tells us, he was succeeded by his son Elah. The latter reigned for less than two years.

His assassination is described above. He was killed whilst in a state of drunkenness in the house of his steward Arza, by Zimri, a senior military officer. It should be noted that Zimri's subsequent reign was the shortest of all the kings of Israel – it only lasted seven days! There was a revolt, and the outcome was that Omri, the commander of the army was proclaimed king. Zimri realised the game was up and committed suicide by burning down the palace with him in it (1 Kings 16:15-20).

Zimri assassinated Elah. This constitutes murder, then and now. His motive was clearly the throne. As did Baasha before him, he coveted the position of king. His plan to effect this could certainly be considered underhand. He waited until Elah was incapacitated by alcohol, so would not have been alert to impending danger and would be unable to adequately defend himself. Additionally, the role of Elah's steward Arza must be open to question here. Was he a co-conspirator? We are not told, but in today's world, the investigating officers would undoubtedly be seeking to clarify this issue.

JEHU

2 Kings 9:14-37

> **Jehu kills Joram and Ahaziah**
>
> So Jehu son of Jehoshaphat, the son of Nimshi, conspired against Joram. (Now Joram and all Israel had been defending Ramoth Gilead against Hazael king of Aram, but king Joram had returned to Jezreel to recover from the wounds the Arameans had inflicted on him in the battle with Hazael king of Aram.) Jehu said, 'If you desire to make me king, don't let anyone slip out of the city to go and tell the news in Jezreel.' Then he got into his chariot and rode to Jezreel, because Joram was resting there and Ahaziah king of Judah had gone down to see him.
>
> When the lookout standing on the tower in Jezreel saw Jehu's troops approaching, he called out, 'I see some troops coming.'
>
> 'Get a horseman,' Joram ordered. 'Send him to meet them and ask, "Do you come in peace?" '
>
> The horseman rode off to meet Jehu and said, 'This is what the king says: 'Do you come in peace?" '
>
> 'What do you have to do with peace?' Jehu replied. 'Fall in behind me.'

The lookout reported, 'The messenger has reached them, but he isn't coming back.'

So the king sent out a second horseman. When he came to them he said, 'This is what the king says: "Do you come in peace?" '

Jehu replied, 'What do you have to do with peace? Fall in behind me.'

The lookout reported, 'He has reached them, but he isn't coming back either. The driving is like that of Jehu son of Nimshi – he drives like a maniac.'

'Hitch up my chariot,' Joram ordered. And when it was hitched up, Joram king of Israel and Ahaziah king of Judah rode out, each in his own chariot, to meet Jehu. They met him at the plot of land that had belonged to Naboth the Jezreelite. When Joram saw Jehu he asked, 'Have you come in peace, Jehu?'

'How can there be peace,' Jehu replied, 'as long as all the idolatry and witchcraft of your mother Jezebel abound?'

Joram turned about and fled, calling out to Ahaziah, 'Treachery, Ahaziah!'

Then Jehu drew his bow and shot Joram between the shoulders. The arrow pierced his heart and he slumped down in his chariot. Jehu said to Bidkar, his chariot officer, 'Pick him up and throw him on the field that belonged to Naboth the Jezreelite. Remember how you and I were riding together in chariots behind Ahab his father when the Lord spoke this prophecy against him: "Yesterday I saw the blood of Naboth and the blood of his sons, declares the Lord, and I will surely make you pay for it on this plot of ground, declares the Lord." Now then, pick him up and throw him on that plot, in accordance with the word of the Lord.'

When Ahaziah king of Judah saw what had happened, he fled up the road to Beth Haggan. Jehu chased him, shouting, 'kill him too!' They wounded him in his chariot on the way up to Gur near Ibleam, but he escaped to Megiddo and died there. His servants took him by chariot to Jerusalem and buried him with his ancestors in his tomb in the city of David. (In the eleventh year of Joram son of Ahab, Ahaziah had become king of Judah.)

Then Jehu went to Jezreel. When Jezebel heard about it, she put on eye make-up, arranged her hair and looked out of a window. As Jehu entered the gate, she asked, 'Have you come in peace, you Zimri, you murderer of your master?'

He looked up at the window and called out, 'Who is on my side? Who?' Two or three eunuchs looked down at him. 'Throw her down!' Jehu said. So they threw her down, and some of her blood spattered the wall and the horses as they trampled her underfoot.

Jehu went in and ate and drank. 'Take care of that cursed woman,' he said, 'and bury her, for she was a king's daughter.' But when they went out to bury her, they found nothing except her skull, her feet and her hands. They went back and told Jehu, who said, 'This is the word of the Lord that he spoke through his servant Elijah the Tishbite: on the plot of ground at Jezreel dogs will devour Jezebel's flesh. Jezebel's body will be like dung on the ground in the plot at Jezreel so that no one will be able to say, "This is Jezebel."'

When it comes to getting rid of royalty, Jehu is your man! He was responsible for killing Joram, king of Israel, Ahaziah, king of Judah, Jezebel, queen of Israel, and around seventy male descendants of Israel's late king Ahab.

He is a very interesting biblical figure. So far as his character traits are concerned, Caldecott[53] notes that:

> One seeks in vain in his character for any touch of magnanimity or of the finer qualities of the ruler. His "zeal for Yahweh" was too much a cloak for merely worldly ambition. The bloodshed in which his rule was founded early provoked a reaction, and his closing years were dark with trouble.

Jehu, at the beginning of this story is an officer with Ahab's bodyguard, and as can be seen from the passage above, was present at the deaths of Naboth and his sons, and also witnessed the encounter between the king and the prophet Elijah, who had pronounced doom on Ahab and his house.

After Ahab's death, his son Ahaziah reigned for a short period and was succeeded by his brother Joram. The latter was seriously wounded in a war with Syria and went to Jezreel to recover. There, he was visited by his friend, King Ahaziah of Judah. In the meantime, Jehu and his fellow senior officers were left in control.

The prophet Elisha, who succeeded Elijah now appears. He would almost certainly know of his predecessor's instruction from God to anoint Hazael as king of Syria, and Jehu as king over Israel (1 Kings 19:15-17). Jehu is anointed as king of Israel and instructed to destroy the house of Ahab and thus avenge the deaths of God's servants who had been killed by Ahab and Jezebel (1 Kings 19:15-17; 2 Kings 9:4-10).

He now sets out for Jezreel with some accompanying horsemen. When the lookout at Jezreel spots him, he tentatively identifies him as Jehu – 'The driving is like that of Jehu son of Nimshi – he drives like a maniac' (2 Kings 9:20). Joram and Ahaziah mount their individual chariots and meet Jehu, ironically, at the plot of ground that had belonged to Naboth. Joram enquires whether Jehu has come in peace, only to be met with a torrent of abuse from Jehu. Although Joram tries to flee, he is lethally wounded by an arrow fired by Jehu.

---

[53] W. S. Caldecott, in *The International Standard Bible Encyclopedia*, Vol. 2, ed. Geoffrey W. Bromiley (Grand Rapids: Eerdmans, 1982), p.982.

Ahaziah is also wounded, and although he reaches Megiddo, his wounds prove fatal.

Jehu now returns to Jezreel where Jezebel insults him by linking him with Zimri's short and disastrous reign (already discussed in this book). Her eunuchs obey his command to throw her down from her window, she is killed, and dogs eat almost all of her body as prophesied by Elijah (1 Kings 21:23).

Two kings and one queen down already, but Jehu still has work to do! The events to date have occurred around Jezreel, but the capital city of Israel was Samaria, where there were 'seventy sons of the house of Ahab' (2 Kings 10:1). They were potential threats to Jehu's desire for the throne, and Jehu, in brief, engineered their deaths at the hands of the city officials.

It should not be forgotten that Jehu also dealt with Jezebel's Baalite legacy. Following the deaths of Jezebel and Ahab's family, he called a convocation ostensibly to celebrate Baal. The prophets, priests, and followers of the false god were all invited, and when all were gathered, he had them killed, the temple of Baal destroyed, and the site turned into a latrine! (2 Kings 10:18-28)

Regrettably, it must also be noted in respect of Jehu, that despite his obedience to God detailed above, that he subsequently fell into apostasy. 2 Kings 10:28-29 tells us that although he destroyed Baal worship in Israel, he worshiped the golden calves at Bethel and Dan which had been placed there by the first king of Israel (the northern kingdom), Jeroboam I.

Before condemning Jehu as a bloodthirsty serial killer (as one might initially be inclined to do), one needs to take a broader view of the whole situation. Jezebel, an adherent of Baal worship, had introduced it into Israel in a big way. Her husband, Ahab, did not resist this incursion of pagan religion into the country. Thus Ahab, and potentially the kingdom, was at best syncretistic in its worship. Yahweh's unique position was suborned. The first commandment was spurned. One might recall here God's covenant with Israel at Sinai. This was the foundation of Israel's existence as the people of God. If they left their God or combined worshipping him with other gods, their whole existence would be in danger.

Both Ahab and Jezebel had been involved in the utterly despicable affair of Naboth's vineyard amongst other nefarious activities which were contrary of the law of God. God's judgement came, using Jehu as his instrument.

JEHOIADA

2 Kings 11:11-18

> The guards, each with weapon in hand, stationed themselves round the king – near the altar and the temple, from the south side to the north side of the temple.
> Jehoiada brought out the king's son and put the crown on him; he presented him with a copy of the covenant and proclaimed him king. They anointed him, and the people clapped their hands and shouted, 'Long live the king!'
>
> When Athaliah heard the noise made by the guards and the people, she went to the people at the temple of the Lord. She looked and there was the king, standing by the pillar, as the custom was. The officers and the trumpeters were beside the king, and all the people of the land were rejoicing and blowing trumpets. Then Athaliah tore her robes and called out, 'Treason! Treason!'
>
> Jehoiada the priest ordered the commanders of units of a hundred, who were in charge of the troops: 'Bring her out between the ranks and put to the sword anyone who follows her.' For the priest had said, 'She must not be put to death in the temple of the Lord.' So they seized her as she reached the place where the horses enter the palace grounds, and there she was put to death.
>
> Jehoiada then made a covenant between the Lord and the king and people that they would be the Lord's people. He also made a covenant between the king and the people. All the people of the land went to the temple of Baal and tore it down. They smashed the altars and idols

to pieces and killed Mattan the priest of Baal in front of the altars.

Before we focus down on this incident, we need to place it in its context for a proper understanding of its content and significance.

Athaliah was from the northern kingdom, Israel. There is some doubt about her exact parentage. The Hebrew word 'daughter' in 2 Kings 8:26 can mean any female descendent, and in the NIV it is translated as 'granddaughter'. It may be more appropriate to consider her as the daughter of Ahab,[54] and she will be regarded as such for our purposes here. She married Jehoram, the son of Jehosaphat, and crown prince of the southern kingdom, Judah. This can be seen as a good political arrangement as it brought together the royal houses of Judah and Israel, but it was a spiritual calamity for Judah.

Aged 32, Jehoram ascended to the throne of Judah and Athaliah became queen. Jehoram then killed all his brothers and other princes, as recorded in 2 Chronicles 21:4. Whether Athaliah was complicit in this is unknown, but a degree of suspicion must exist.

The northern court was devoted to the false Canaanite god, Baal, and she introduced the worship of Baal to the southern kingdom in Jerusalem. In 2 Chronicles 22:3 we find her blamed for her son's bad deeds: 'He too followed the ways of the house of Ahab, for his mother encouraged him to act wickedly'. Indeed, in 2 Chronicles 24:7 we learn that 'the sons of that wicked woman Athaliah had broken into the temple of God and had used even its sacred objects for the Baals'.

Jehoram died fighting the Edomites and their son Ahaziah became king, but only reigned for one year, dying from wounds inflicted by Jehu, as already documented in this book. The lady seems to have had a thirst for power and she emphatically did not want to be deprived of it. She slaughtered the royal household, all except for Ahaziah's infant son Joash. He and his nurse were hidden and thus

[54] W. S. Caldicott and D. F. Payne, in *The International Standard Bible Encyclopedia*, Vol. 1, ed. Geoffrey W. Bromiley (Grand Rapids: Eerdmans, 1979), p.349-350.

preserved by Jehosheba, the aunt of Joash (2 Kings 11:2; 2 Chronicles 22:11).

Athaliah, thinking that all potential competition for the throne had been obliterated, had herself declared sovereign. Little did she know that for six years Joash had been cared for in hiding by Jehosheba and her priest husband, Jehoiada. He was the chief priest of the Jerusalem temple during the reigns of Ahaziah, Athaliah and Joash. As already noted, he married Jehosheba, who was the sister of King Ahaziah. After hiding Joash in the temple precincts for six years, he brought him out of hiding to proclaim him as the rightful king, as the passage above describes.

It is certainly worth noting carefully the last paragraph of the biblical account reproduced above. A covenant is made 'between the Lord and the king and people.' Jehoiada was clearly aiming at the apostasy which had occurred under the leadership of Athalaiah, and was seeking to bring the nation, from the king down, back under the authority of God. This is emphasised by the consequent abrogation of any affinity to the worship of Baal by the people destroying his temple and killing his priest. Jehoiada had drawn a line in the sand.

Although our primary interest here is the instigation of Athaliah's death by Jehoida, it is appropriate also to make comment on the other deaths mentioned in connection with this story.

Athaliah had usurped the throne. She was not the legitimate monarch. Her propounding of a false religion rendered her liable to death under Old Testament law. Her killing of the royal household constituted murder. When her son, Ahaziah, was killed by Jehu, her grandchildren were the only impediment between her and the throne. She mercilessly killed them (with the exception, as already learned, of Joash).

The ruthless and merciless behaviour of Athaliah might inspire some speculation concerning the nature of her personality. One might speculate as to whether it contained elements compatible with a diagnosis of severe personality disorder. Here is not the place to engage in a technical discussion on personality disorder, nor does the Bible provide adequate information (at least in most cases) for modern classificatory purposes, but this is an area to which a forensic psychiatrist of today would address much thought in the preparation of a court report.

Despite all the horror of Athaliah, it is cheering to note that the story does have a happy ending! There was a renewal of the covenant, as reported in 2 Kings 11:17. The Deuteronomic covenant between the people and God was back in place. The legitimate dynasty was back on the throne. Grounds for optimism! (At least for now.)

Discussion

In our small group of perpetrators here, there is a variety of motivation. Baasha and Zimri can be seen to act out of self-interest, whereas Jehoida, Jehu, and Samuel were, either directly or indirectly, fulfilling the will of God.

Both Baasha and Zimri are unattractive characters. They wanted power, to be the head of state, or perhaps more accurately, the despot. The essential root of this untoward desire is jealousy. One can also detect a degree of grandiosity in their thinking. *They* were the individuals who were most suited to executive power – not the lesser mortals currently occupying the position. They envied the current rulers and plotted their violent downfall. These were not spontaneous acts on their part, but the consequence of careful planning.

We have but little by way of detail in terms of Baasha's act of assassination other than it took place in the context of military operations. Zimri's killing of Elah took place when the latter was in the house of Arza, a palace official, and occurred when Elah was incapacitated by alcohol. Both Baasha and Zimri killed the families of their predecessors. One might well think that both (and Athaliah for that matter) had undesirable character traits, for example those of dissocial personality disorder (akin to psychopathic disorder in previous classificatory systems). For interest, such a disorder is characterised by the following:[55]

(a) callous unconcern for the feelings of others;

[55] *The ICD-10 Classification of Mental and Behavioural Disorders* (Geneva: WHO, 1992), p.204.

(b) gross and persistent attitude of irresponsibility and disregard for social norms, rules and obligations;
(c) incapacity to maintain enduring relationships, though having no difficulty in establishing them;
(d) very low tolerance to frustration and a low threshold for discharge of aggression, including violence;
(e) incapacity to experience guilt or to profit from experience, particularly punishment;
(f) marked proneness to blame others, or to offer plausible rationalizations, for the behaviour that has brought the patient into conflict with society.

We can by no means just look at the above-described features and use them as tick boxes. First, it should be noted that they are applicable to our society today. They cannot necessarily be applied indiscriminately to a different society with a very different culture to that which currently pertains. We may be horrified that the families of the deceased monarchs were murdered, but that was standard practice at the time in order to preclude other (and arguably more legitimate) claims being made to the throne.

Nevertheless, to transport Baasha and Zimri into today's world, if they were facing murder charges for the deaths of their predecessors, psychiatrists both for the prosecution and the defence would undoubtedly be concentrating their minds on whether personality disorder was present, and if so, whether this could be considered as an abnormality of mind which substantially impaired the accused's ability for his acts and omissions. If the jury found this to be the case, the conviction would be one for manslaughter rather than murder, and the judge's sentencing options much broadened compared with the otherwise mandatory life sentence.

Turning next to Jehoiada, as has already been shown, Athaliah was not a legitimate ruler. She was not of the Davidic dynasty, but an Omride (of the house of Omri). Also, she was a woman, and in Israel, executive power was exclusive to the male line. Jehoiada's motive is thus clear. He was restoring the throne to the God-appointed line of succession. His motivation is confirmed in 2 Kings 11:17-20 when subsequent destruction and blood-letting is for the purpose of confirming the people as God's people and reaffirming their covenant relationship:

> Jehoiada then made a covenant between the Lord and the king and people that they would be the Lord's people. He also made a covenant between the king and the people. All the people of the land went to the temple of Baal and tore it down. They smashed the altars and idols in pieces and killed Mattan the priest of Baal in front of the altars.
>
> Then Jehoiada the priest posted guards at the temple of the Lord. He took with him the commanders of hundreds, the Carites, the guards and all the people of the land, and together they brought the king down from the temple of the Lord and went into the palace, entering by way of the gate of the guards. The king then took his place on the royal throne. All the people of the land rejoiced, and the city was calm, because Athaliah had been slain with the sword at the palace.

Konkel[56] provides an apt end-note to this story:

> The restoration of a true Davidite king and the death of Athaliah bring an end to the domination of the Baal cult in Judah.

Saul has refused to kill Agag (despite the unequivocal divine command in Deuteronomy 25:19). It is left to Samuel to enact God's command. The consequences of rank disobedience were catastrophic for Saul, as already noted. Once again, it is clear that God's purpose cannot be thwarted (Job 42:2).

Jehu, like Jehoiada and Samuel before him, was an instrument of God, bringing retribution for the death of Naboth, destroying the house of Ahab, and destroying the Baalites. Nonetheless, he was a flawed character in that he subsequently apostatised.

Despite the varied motives involved in these regicides, one can discern one central unifying theme. Adherence to the will, and commands, of God leads to contentment. Attempts to thwart God's decreed will are destined to culminate in ruination.

---

[56] August H. Konkel, *1 & 2 Kings*, NIVAC (Grand Rapids: Zondervan, 2006).

Chapter Seven
JEALOUSY

Introduction

Many readers of this book will have some familiarity with Shakespeare's play 'Othello'. Very briefly, Othello is a general in the Venetian army. He has recently married Desdemona, a beautiful lady from a prestigious family. Iago is his ensign and is angry because he thinks Othello has passed him over for promotion, instead appointing Cassio as his lieutenant. Malevolently, Iago plants doubt in Othello's mind about his wife's sexual fidelity, suggesting she is being unfaithful to him with Cassio. Othelllo murders Desdemona, and on finding he has been lied to, commits suicide over her body.

Sexual jealousy as a motive for murder is, as they say, as old as the hills. Spouses/partners are unfaithful. Spouses/partners are killed as a result. As a forensic psychiatrist, my main professional interest here is in a small part of this general area, specifically, what is in diagnostic terms called morbid jealousy. This is a (fortunately) uncommon condition where there is no reason for the partner to be jealous, but the jealous beliefs are the consequence of illness. The affected individual is almost always a male (and will so be referred to from this point on, for the sake of convenience), and suffers from a single delusion, specifically that his wife/partner is being unfaithful to him. He will often go to great lengths to substantiate his false belief, for example, following her, checking her mobile phone, computer records, and many other things. Often he will persistently bombard her with questions about where she has been, who she has seen, etcetera, in order to elicit a confession of infidelity. Worn down by incessant questioning, and in order to try and obtain some peace, the woman will sometimes falsely admit to the accusations. This is something you should NOT do in these circumstances, for the man, now feeling vindicated, often then proceeds to kill her. Forensic psychiatrists should always be consulted if morbid jealousy is suspected. Regrettably, this diagnosis often only emerges after the woman has been killed, and the man is being examined for the purpose of providing a court report in a murder charge case (all murder charges are examined pre-trial by at least one psychiatrist for the purpose of providing a psychiatric report to the court). I recall one of my cases in a maximum secure hospital many years ago. He was a nurse, and presented as being of pleasant and inoffensive character. He had killed his wife, having the delusion she was being unfaithful to him, and stabbed her seventy-odd times.

Although cases where people have been killed through a motive of jealousy (whether morbid or not) often attract extensive media coverage, this motive is often to the fore in more mundane offending. Jealousy, and its close relative, envy (covetousness), are at the root of a wide range of criminal behaviour, and this is often forgotten or ignored. The criminal damage to a Rolls Royce is often enacted because the perpetrator resents the fact that the owner can afford such an expensive car, and they cannot. They do not go round keying old bangers. They do so out of jealousy. Even a mugger or a burglar can be viewed as acting out of envy, at least in large part. The victim has something or things that the criminal wants, and is prepared to offend to get them. Even if the motivation on the surface is more direct – they want money for drugs – the element of envy is still present. Establishing motivation for a criminal offence is not necessarily as straightforward as it might appear at first sight.

Indeed, the complexity of motive at times is well illustrated by the five occurrences in the Bible considered in this section. They are all cases where jealousy was involved to a greater or lesser extent, yet they are all very different in the ways in which this played out. Death occurred in all cases other than that of Joseph's brothers, yet there too death was the original intended result in at least most of their minds.

Jealousy's malign finger is present in much sinful behaviour. It might not be the most obvious motivational factor, but even though not immediately obvious, when one pries below the surface its malign presence can become apparent.

CAIN

Genesis 4:1-16

Adam made love to his wife Eve, and she became pregnant and gave birth to Cain. She said, 'With the help of the Lord I have brought forth a man. Later she gave birth to his brother Abel.

Now Abel kept flocks, and Cain worked the soil. In the course of time Cain brought some of the fruits of the soil as an offering to the Lord. But Abel also brought an offering – fat portions from some of the firstborn of his flock. The Lord looked with favour on Abel and his offering, but on Cain and his offering he did not look with favour. So Cain was very angry, and his face was downcast.

Then the Lord said to Cain, 'Why are you angry? Why is your face downcast? If you do what is right, will you not be accepted? But if you do not do what is right, sin is crouching at your door; it desires to have you, but you must rule over it'.

Now Cain said to his brother Abel, 'Let's go out to the field.' While they were in the field, Cain attacked his brother Abel and killed him.

Then the Lord said to Cain, 'Where is your brother Abel?'

'I don't know,' he replied. 'Am I my brother's keeper?'

The Lord said, 'What have you done? Listen! Your brother's blood cries out to me from the ground. Now you are under a curse and driven from the ground which opened its mouth to receive your brother's blood from your hand. When you work the ground, it will no longer yield its crops for you. You will be a restless wanderer on the earth.'

> Cain said to the Lord, 'my punishment is more than I can bear. Today you are driving me from the land, and I will be hidden from your presence; I will be a restless wanderer on the earth, and whoever finds me will kill me.'
>
> But the Lord said to him, 'Not so; anyone who kills Cain will suffer vengeance seven times over.' Then the Lord put a mark on Cain so that no one who found him would kill him. So Cain went out from the Lord's presence and lived in the land of Nod, east of Eden.

Before turning directly to the contents of the above passage, it is worth remembering that the connection between God and the first man and woman was damaged by the introduction of sin into the world (the 'vertical' line), and that this resulted in a damaged relationship between people (the 'horizontal' line). The early chapters of Genesis thus set the scene of what has been so often repeated in history: sin against God and against one's neighbour. It should also be emphasised here that God's grace is visible from the beginning: he makes clothes for Adam and Eve, and protects Cain by a sign.

The biblical account of Cain's slaying of Abel is well known, albeit arguably not always well understood. Indeed, there are a number of difficulties here, and in more than one area. The account clearly has more in terms of its content, both explicit and implied, than is appreciated at a first brief reading. There are also issues surrounding the translation of the Hebrew text, and these are helpfully alluded to by Hamilton.[57] The belief that Cain's sacrificial offering was unacceptable because it was not a blood sacrifice is still popularly held (albeit not a view which has been espoused by any major commentary from evangelical circles in many years). Arguably a more compelling explanation is based on the hearts of Abel and Cain in their approach to worship. Abel's offering was 'fat portions from some of the firstborn of his flock'. That of Cain was 'some of the fruits of the soil'. In giving fat from the firstborn Abel was giving of the best available to him. This sense is not implied by the description

---

[57] Victor P. Hamilton, *The Book of Genesis Chapters 1-17*, NICOT (Grand Rapids: Eerdmans, 1990), p.269,272.

of Cain's offering. Cain's heart did not dictate that he offered the best available to God, Abel's did.

The outline of events is straightforward and brief. Cain is the first child born to Adam and Eve. Abel is born later. Cain grew crops, and Abel kept livestock. Both brought sacrificial offerings to the Lord, but whereas those of Abel were looked on with favour, those of Cain were not. In consequence, Cain is described as 'very angry, and his face was downcast' (v.5). God asked him why this was so and told him that if he did what was right, he would be accepted. Cain's response is to suggest to his brother that they go out to the field, whereupon Cain kills him. God then tells Cain that he is under a curse. Cain is worried that he will be killed, but God placed a mark on him to preclude this. Subsequently, Cain fathered a child and founded a dynasty.

There can be no doubt that in today's world Cain's actions constitute murder. He resents the fact that Abel's sacrifice is acceptable and his is not. Such is his furious response that he inveigles Abel to an open space where he attacks and kills him. He had a grievance against his brother on the basis of the acceptability of their individual offerings, specifically because his was found to be wanting. There can be no doubt that his murderous attack was pre-planned – he invited Abel out to the field, where, presumably, they would be unobserved.

When one considers motivation, one should probably bear in mind Sailhamer's[58] comment that:

> Rather than attempting to discover what was wrong with Cain's offering, we would be better advised simply to take notice that the author has omitted any explanation. He was apparently less concerned about Cain's offering than he was about Cain's response to the Lord's rejection of his offering.

One would not wish to be over-speculative in a situation where the Bible is silent, but it might well be the case that at least in part, Cain

---

[58] John H. Sailhamer, in The Expositor's Bible Commentary, Vol. 1, ed. Frank E. Gaebelein (Grand Rapids: Zondervan, 1990), p.61.

acted from jealousy in his fratricide (the killing of a brother). Abel's sacrifice was acceptable to God. That of Cain was not.

JOSEPH'S BROTHERS

Genesis 37:17-28

> So Joseph went after his brothers and found them near Dothan. But they saw him in the distance, and before he reached them, they plotted to kill him.
>
> 'Here comes that dreamer!' they said to each other. 'Come now, let's kill him and throw him into one of these cisterns and say that a ferocious animal devoured him. Then we'll see what comes of his dreams.'
>
> When Reuben heard this, he tried to rescue him from their hands. 'let's not take his life,' he said. 'Don't shed any blood. Throw him into this cistern here in the wilderness, but don't lay a hand on him.' Reuben said this to rescue him from them and take him back to his father.
>
> So when Joseph came to his brothers, they stripped him of his robe – the ornate robe he was wearing – and they took him and threw him into the cistern. The cistern was empty; there was no water in it.
>
> As they sat down to eat their meal, they looked up and saw a caravan of Ishmaelites coming from Gilead. Their camels were loaded with spices, balm and myrrh, and they were on their way to take them down to Egypt.
>
> Judah said to his brothers, 'What will we gain if we kill our brother and cover up his blood? Come, let's sell him to the Ishmaelites and not lay our hands on him; after all, he is our brother, our own flesh and blood.' His brothers agreed.
>
> So when the Midianite merchants came by, his brothers pulled Joseph up out of the cistern and sold him for

> twenty shekels of silver to the Ishmaelites, who took him to Egypt.

To properly appreciate the nuances of this story it is a necessary precursor to be aware of the background family history.

The brothers' father, Jacob, loved Laban's younger daughter Rachel, but was tricked by her father into marrying her less attractive sister Leah as well. Of the brothers, Leah was mother to Reuben, Simeon, Levi, Judah, Issachar, and Zebulun. Additionally, she had a daughter, Dinah, who appears in another part of this book. Her maid, Zilpah bore Gad and Asher to Jacob, who also fathered Dan and Naphtali by Rachel's maid Bilhah. Joseph was the youngest of these and was born to Jacob's favoured wife, Rachel (who had previously had problems conceiving). Because of this, Jacob 'loved Joseph more than any of his other sons, because he had been born to him in his old age; and he made an ornate robe for him' (Genesis 37:3).

What the NIV translates as 'ornate robe' is often referred to by its KJV designation as a coat of many colours. Whatever its nature, it was clearly distinctive, and almost certainly expensive. That Joseph, despite being younger and hence in the normal cultural mores of that day, of lesser importance, was almost paradoxically the favourite son, was patently obvious, and the other brothers deeply resented what they saw as gross preferment. Indeed, Genesis 37:4 tells us that 'they hated him and could not speak a kind word to him'.

To aggravate a tense situation even further, Joseph then has two dreams, the contents of both he communicates to his brothers. Both involve the members of the family offering homage to Joseph! Unsurprisingly the brothers hate him even more (v.8). They are jealous of him (v.11).

In terms of the immediate background to the passage quoted at the beginning of this chapter, the brothers are away from home grazing the flocks. Jacob instructs Joseph to go and check that all is well with them and the flock. Joseph eventually tracks down their whereabouts and meets up with them at Dothan.

It is clear from the biblical account that, even from seeing Joseph in the distance, his brothers' intention was to effect his death, and this gives a good idea of their feelings towards him. Whereas their options would undoubtedly have been limited at home, in the presence of their father, out here in open country opportunity is knocking, and they seize it with both hands. They formulate what sounds to be a viable plan, and one which is unlikely to engender suspicion when relayed to their father.

Reuben, the oldest brother, clearly less inclined than the others to the shedding of blood, comes up with a non-violent alternative plan. He suggests incarcerating Joseph in a dry water cistern, with the intention of rescuing him later and effecting his return home. Joseph is thrown into the cistern, having first been stripped of his robe, whereupon Ishmaelite traders appear, and Judah comes up with the idea of solving the problem without bloodshed by selling their brother to them. The traders were transporting their wares to Egypt, and such a course of action would essentially mean consigning Joseph to slavery there.

And so it was done.

The brothers have acted in an odious manner towards Joseph, who, despite not sharing a mother with any of them is still their half-brother. Reuben comes out of this sorry tale better than the others – he at least is planning to rescue Joseph and return him to his father's home. Judah suggests a non-fatal solution, and this is the one selected. Joseph keeps his life but is condemned to potential life-long slavery in Egypt. Blood has not been shed, but it so easily could have been.

In modern day law, a number of offences have been committed here. Conspiracy to murder probably tops the list, but when one includes their subsequent account to their father, they are guilty of lying. In modern UK law, slavery is a criminal offence under the Modern Slavery Act 2015 (MSA 2015) and carries a maximum sentence of life imprisonment. Facing court today, Joseph's brothers would undoubtedly be facing a long stretch!

We know the eventual outcome of this seemingly catastrophic life event for Joseph. He is transported to Egypt where he becomes Potiphar's slave, is imprisoned following false accusations by Potiphar's wife, interprets Pharaoh's dreams, and ends up being a ruler, second only to the authority of Pharaoh! He meets up with his brothers again when they travel to Egypt to buy food in a time of famine.

Reconciliation takes place and it is in this context that Joseph voices the well-known words of Genesis 50:20:

> You intended to harm me, but God intended it for good to accomplish what is now being done, the saving of many lives.

A salutary reminder, if one is necessary, of the providence of God.

DAVID

2 Samuel 11:1-27

> In the spring, at the time when kings go off to war, David sent Joab out with the king's men and the whole Israelite army. They destroyed the Ammonites and besieged Rabbah. But David remained in Jerusalem.
>
> One evening David got up from his bed and walked around on the roof of the palace. From the roof he saw a woman washing. The woman was very beautiful, and David sent someone to find out about her. The man said, 'She is Bathsheba, the daughter of Eliam and the wife of Uriah the Hittite.' Then David sent messengers to get her. She came to him, and he slept with her. (Now she was purifying herself from her monthly uncleanness.) Then she went back home. The woman conceived and sent word to David, saying, 'I am pregnant.'
>
> So David sent this word to Joab: 'Send me Uriah the Hittite.' And Joab sent him to David. When Uriah came to him, David asked him how Joab was, how the soldiers were and how the war was going. Then David said to Uriah, 'Go down to your house and wash your feet.' So Uriah left the palace, and a gift from the king was sent after him. But Uriah slept at the entrance to the palace

with all his master's servants and did not go down to his house.

David was told, 'Uriah did not go home.' So he asked Uriah, 'Haven't you just come from a military campaign? Why didn't you go home?'

Uriah said to David, 'The ark and Israel and Judah are staying in tents, and my commander Joab and my lord's men are camped in the open country. How could I go to my house to eat and drink and make love to my wife? As surely as you live, I will not do such a thing!'

Then David said to him, 'Stay here one more day, and tomorrow I will send you back.' So Uriah remained in Jerusalem that day and the next. At David's invitation, he ate and drank with him, and David made him drunk. But in the evening Uriah went out to sleep on his mat among his master's servants; he did not go home.

In the morning David wrote a letter to Joab and sent it with Uriah. In it he wrote, 'Put Uriah out in front where the fighting is fiercest. Then withdraw from him so that he will be struck down and die.'

So while Joab had the city under siege, he put Uriah at a place where he knew the strongest defenders were. When the men of the city came out and fought against Joab, some of the men in David's army fell; moreover, Uriah the Hittite died.

Joab sent David a full account of the battle. He instructed the messenger: 'When you have finished giving the king this account of the battle, the king's anger may flare up, and he may ask you, "Why did you get so close to the city to fight? Didn't you know they would shoot arrows from the wall? Who killed Abimelek son of Jerub-Besheth? Didn't a woman drop an upper millstone on him from the wall, so that he died in Thebez? Why did you get so close to the wall?' If he asks you this, then say to him, "Moreover, your servant Uriah the Hittite is dead."'

The messenger set out, and when he arrived he told David everything Joab had sent him to say. The messenger said to David, 'The men overpowered us and came out against us in the open, but we drove them back to the entrance of the city gate. Then the archers shot arrows at your servants from the wall, and some of the king's men died. Moreover, your servant Uriah the Hittite is dead.'

David told the messenger, 'Say this to Joab: "Don't let this upset you; the sword devours one as well as another. Press the attack against the city and destroy it." Say this to encourage Joab.'

When Uriah's wife heard that her husband was dead, she mourned for him. After the time of mourning was over, David had her brought to his house, and she became his wife and bore him a son. But the thing David had done displeased the Lord.

This story is a prime example of how the sin of covetousness can lead to further serious sin. David coveted Uriah's wife, and this culminated in him effecting the death of Uriah.

The beginning of the biblical account, reproduced above, contextualises this pericope. The time is spring, when kings go out to battle. In the ANE (Ancient Near East), there was a season for going to war and the spring was when it started. This has been a common practice throughout much of history, and the tradition was followed by the Romans, amongst others. There are obvious practical considerations which underpin such practice.

In terms of place, David is in his palace in Jerusalem. This is remarkable because his army under Joab, its commander, is in the field, at war with the Ammonites. One would expect David as commander-in-chief to be with his troops, as convention dictated. Instead, he is enjoying all the comforts of his position and palace while his troops rough it in a military camp.

One day, from the roof of his palace, he sees a stunning woman bathing. He is filled with lustful thoughts towards her. He sends messengers to bring her to him and has sexual relations with her. Here we are not told whether the woman (Bathsheba) was consenting to their sexual activity. It should be borne in mind that if David sent for her, this would have constituted a royal command, and thus something which had to be obeyed. The presence or absence of willingness on her part to engage in sexual relations at this point must remain a matter for conjecture. She later discovers that as a result of this tryst that she is pregnant and sends word to this effect to David. That she was not pregnant prior to her encounter with David is made explicit by the author from the statement that 'she was purifying herself from her monthly uncleanness' (2 Samuel 11:4). It should be noted that the evidence that she was carrying a child would not have been apparent for a number of weeks.

David is now in a calamitous situation. Bathsheba is pregnant, and this cannot be the child of her husband Uriah who is and was away on active service at the time of conception. He appears to have been a senior officer in the army. What will happen when this becomes common knowledge? What will Uriah do? What effect will it have on morale in the army? What will be the consequences for his kingly authority? All these and other questions likely went through David's mind when he considered this potentially disastrous predicament.

What is he to do?

David recalls Uriah to Jerusalem, and after some small talk about the troops and the war, tells him to go home and 'wash your feet' (v. 8). This is a euphemism. The word 'feet' could be used in the Hebrew language to refer to the genitals, and what David was actually suggesting was that Uriah go home and have sexual relations with his wife. This would provide a legitimate and understandable explanation for her pregnancy!

Unfortunately for David, Uriah has strong moral scruples. He is still on active service, and he does not feel he can go home and enjoy himself while his military colleagues are suffering the privations of waging war. Uriah doesn't go home. David's initial plan is scuppered, so on to plan two. David tells Uriah to stay another night, and on the next day invites him for a meal where he plies him with copious amounts of alcohol, rendering Uriah drunk, doubtless thinking that this will diminish his moral scruples and result in him going home to make love to his wife. It doesn't! David must have been becoming desperate at this point and devises a shocking plan three. He sends a missive to Joab instructing him to effect Uriah's death in battle. Ironically it is Uriah himself who carries his death warrant back to the field of operations.

David's final and nefarious stratagem is successfully enacted, and Uriah's death is realised. David marries Bathsheba and their son is born, only to die a few days later.

In today's legal situation the position is clear. David conspired to murder Uriah. He would be so charged and would have no credible defence. The motive is clear – to conceal his infidelity with Bathsheba, Uriah's wife, and to prevent disgrace to him. Joab would also face a similar charge as he was complicit in the plot with David.

In David's own age, Israel, as noted elsewhere in this book, was a theocracy. Its ultimate authority was God, not the king, and God's law, as documented in the Pentateuch was broken. He has violated at least three of the ten commandments as documented in Exodus 20 and Deuteronomy 5. He has committed murder, adultery, and coveted his neighbour's wife. The penalty for murder was death (Exodus 21:12), and likewise for adultery (Leviticus 20:10).

2 Samuel 11:27b informs that 'the thing David had done displeased the Lord'. That David recognised his sin and repented is clear from Psalm 51:4, 'Against you, you only, have I sinned and done what is evil in your sight'. Nevertheless, from this point on, David's life changed. Previously he had lived what seems, in the vernacular, almost a charmed life. From this point on the consequences of his sin are apparent, with problems, particularly in the context of his own family.

We may be forgiven for our transgressions, but the repercussions can come back to haunt us in later life.

JEZEBEL

1 Kings 21:1-16

Some time later there was an incident involving a vineyard belonging to Naboth the Jezreelite. The vineyard was in Jezreel, close to the palace of Ahab king of Samaria. Ahab said to Naboth, 'Let me have your vineyard to use for a vegetable garden, since it is close to my palace. In exchange I will give you a better vineyard or, if you prefer, I will pay you whatever it is worth.' But Naboth replied, 'The Lord forbid that I should give you the inheritance of my ancestors.' So Ahab went home, sullen and angry because Naboth the Jezreelite had said, 'I will not give you the inheritance of my ancestors.' He lay on his bed sulking and refused to eat.

His wife Jezebel came in and asked him, 'Why are you so sullen? Why won't you eat?' He answered her, 'Because I said to Naboth the Jezreelite, 'Sell me your vineyard; or if you prefer, I will give you another vineyard in its place.' But he said, "I will not give you my vineyard,' 'Jezebel his wife said, 'Is this how you act as king over Israel? Get up and eat! Cheer up. I'll get you the vineyard of Naboth the Jezreelite.'

So she wrote letters in Ahab's name, placed his seal on them, and sent them to the elders and nobles who lived in Naboth's city with him. In those letters she wrote:

'Proclaim a day of fasting and give Naboth a prominent seat among the people. But put two scoundrels opposite him and get them to bring charges that he has cursed both God and the king. Then take him out and stone him to death.'

So the elders and nobles who lived in Naboth's city did as Jezebel directed in the letters she had written to them, They proclaimed a fast and seated Naboth in a prominent place among the people. Then two scoundrels came and

> sat opposite him and brought charges against Naboth before the people, saying, 'Naboth has cursed both God and the king.' So they took him outside the city and stoned him to death. Then they sent word to Jezebel: 'Naboth has been stoned to death.'
>
> As soon as Jezebel heard that Naboth had been stoned to death, she said to Ahab, 'Get up and take possession of the vineyard of Naboth the Jezreelite that he refused to sell you. He is no longer alive, but dead.' When Ahab heard that Naboth was dead, he got up and went down to take possession of Naboth's vineyard.

Ahab was king of Israel, the northern kingdom. It will be remembered that following the death of Solomon, the kingdom divided into the northern kingdom (Israel), and the southern kingdom (Judah) in 930 BC. He reigned for 22 years between 874 and 853 BC, following the death of his father Omri. He married a foreigner, Jezebel. She was a malevolent influence on her husband and the kingdom in general. She was the daughter of King Ethbaal of Sidon and brought her pagan religion with her. Indeed, 1 Kings 16:31 informs of Ahab that 'he also married Jezebel daughter of Ethbaal king of the Sidonians, and began to serve Baal and worship him'. It will be recalled that this is the same woman who is recorded as trying to destroy all of the prophets of the one true God in the country (1 Kings 18:4) and replacing the worship of God with that of Baal and his consort Asherah (1 Kings 18:19). These latter prophets were shown to be false by Elijah on Mount Carmel (1 Kings 18), when God sent down fire to consume Elijah's water-soaked sacrifice. Unsurprisingly this infuriated Jezebel, and Elijah had to flee for his life. It is thus clear from the start that Jezebel is an enemy of God and his servants. Her influence over her husband appears to have been strong, and malign.

The other main figure in this drama is an Israelite farmer called Naboth. He owned a vineyard in the Jezreel Valley adjacent to the palace of Ahab. Nothing else is known of him, although it can be inferred from his actions that he was God-fearing.

Ahab wants Naboth's vineyard to turn it into a vegetable garden, presumably because of its proximity to his palace. He commences negotiations with Naboth in an amicable and reasonable manner. He offers him either a better vineyard elsewhere, or the value of the land in cash. Naboth's response is to tell the king, 'The Lord forbid that I should give you the inheritance of my ancestors' (1 Kings 21:3). Here, Naboth is referring to Leviticus 25:23 in which God states that, 'The land must not be sold permanently, because the land is mine and you reside in my land as foreigners and strangers'. Even lease of the land could only take place until the Jubilee year (Leviticus 25:15-16). Naboth knew the law of God and was determined to adhere to it. Ahab should have known it, and most probably did!

Ahab goes home in a very bad mood – 'sullen and angry' according to 1 Kings 21:4. It goes on to say that 'he lay on his bed sulking and refused to eat'. His response to the rejection of his offer presents as being rather childish. It does not impress as the reaction of a monarch. When his wife sees him in this mood, she inquires as to the reason, and when he tells her, she is much more proactive. She briskly retorts, 'Is this how you act as king over Israel? Get up and eat! Cheer up. I'll get you the vineyard of Naboth the Jezreelite' (1 Kings 21:7). As opposed to Ahab's sulks, Jezebel is action woman!

True to her word, Jezebel springs into activity. Using the king's name and his seal she writes to notable figures in Naboth's home city and tells them to have a day of fasting, give Naboth a prominent place, and then send for two good-for-nothings to accuse him of blaspheming both God and the king, to be followed by his stoning to death. And so it happens.

When the news reaches Jezebel, she tells the king of Naboth's decease and he takes possession of the vineyard of the deceased. Mission accomplished!

This is not the end of the story for God's judgement will follow.

Jezebel did not cast the stones that dispatched Naboth. Nonetheless, she contrived to have him put to death by others. Those to whom she wrote would have had no doubt but that they, by following her orders (although they would have thought that they came from the king), were acting in a criminal manner. They were to obtain false testimony as a pretext for the execution of a blameless citizen of their city. One might argue here that they were obliged to obey the orders which emanated from the throne, but any such claim does not bear scrutiny. The Israelites were under Mosaic law, the law which God had communicated at Mount Sinai following the exodus from Egypt. The ninth commandment states, 'You shall not give false testimony against your neighbour', and the sixth, 'You shall not murder' (Exodus 20:13,16). Additionally, the strictures against false testimony are made clear in Deuteronomy 19:16-21.

In English common law the offence of conspiracy is committed when two or more people agree to 'do an unlawful act, or to do a lawful act by unlawful means' (*Mulcahy* (1868) LR3 HL 306). There can be no doubt that Jezebel and those she instructed committed conspiracy to murder.

This was not the twentieth century, and no formal legal process took place. Yet there should have been a formal legal process in the way Mosaic law prescribed. Israel had a unique system of justice and even a king was subject to it.

Nevertheless, Elijah's prophecy of 1 Kings 21:23 that, 'Dogs will devour Jezebel by the wall of Jezreel' was to be fulfilled (2 Kings 9:30-37). The demands of justice were satisfied.

XERXES

Esther 7:1-10

> So the king and Haman went to Queen Esther's banquet, and as they were drinking wine on the second day, the king again asked, 'Queen Esther, what is your petition? It will be given you. What is your request? Even up to half the kingdom, it will be granted.'
>
> Then Queen Esther answered, 'If I have found favour with you, Your Majesty, and if it pleases you, grant me my life – this is my petition. And spare my people – this is my request. For I and my people have been sold to be destroyed, killed and annihilated. If we had merely been sold as male and female slaves, I would have kept quiet, because no such distress would justify disturbing the king.'

> King Xerxes asked Queen Esther, 'Who is he? Where is he – the man who has dared to do such a thing?'
>
> Esther said, 'An adversary and enemy! This vile Haman!'
>
> Then Haman was terrified before the king and queen. The king got up in a rage, left his wine and went out into the palace garden. But Haman, realising that the king had already decided his fate, stayed behind to beg Queen Esther for his life.
>
> Just as the king returned from the palace garden to the banqueting hall, Haman was falling on the couch where Esther was reclining.
>
> The king exclaimed, 'Will he even molest the queen while she is with me in the house?'
>
> As soon as the word left the king's mouth, they covered Haman's face. Then Harbona, one of the eunuchs attending the king, said, 'A pole reaching to a height of fifty cubits stands by Haman's house. He had it set up for Mordecai, who spoke up to help the king.
>
> The king said, 'Impale him on it!' So they impaled Haman on the pole he had set up for Mordecai. Then the king's fury subsided.

The story of Esther is well known, perhaps especially well in Jewish circles, as it forms the basis of the festival of Purim. This is a time of audience participation in the synagogue. The book of Esther is read, and whenever the name of Haman is mentioned, the congregation enthusiastically shouts and boos!

It is relevant to briefly recapitulate the events leading up to the biblical passage quoted above.

The events take place in and around the royal palace of the Persian king, Xerxes (called Ahasuerus in some translations), at Susa, the chief of four capital cities used by Persian monarchs. Xerxes has divorced his wife, Vashti, following her reluctance to obey his command to appear as his trophy wife at a banquet of men who were intoxicated with alcohol to a greater or lesser extent.

Xerxes now has a vacancy for a queen, and his staff engage in a detailed search for a suitable candidate. Esther is eventually selected by Xerxes and the position is very satisfactorily filled! Indeed, she 'had a lovely figure and was beautiful' (Est. 2:7), and 'the king was attracted to Esther more than to any of the other women, and she won his favour and approval more than any of the other virgins' (Esther 2:17).

Esther was of Jewish ethnicity, the daughter of a Benjamite named Abihail. Her ancestor Kish was one of the prisoners taken from Jerusalem by Nebuchadnezzar when he sacked it in 586/7 BC. At some point she was orphaned, and subsequently brought up by her cousin Mordecai, who held a post in the palace (Esther 2:5-7). It is important to note that when the king married her, he was not aware of her racial background. Mordecai had forbidden her to disclose this (Esther 2:10).

Haman is the villain of the story. He is described as an Agagite, suggesting he was descended from the Amalekite king, Agag, whom Saul neglected to kill in 1 Samuel 15. There was a history of long-standing enmity between the Amalekites and the Israelites (Exodus 17:8-16; Deuteronomy 25:17-19; 1 Chronicles 4:43). Haman was determined to revive this old tradition! He was incensed at the refusal of Mordecai to show him obeisance by kneeling or bowing before him. His vituperative hatred of the Jewish people as a nation expressed itself in his successful manoeuvring the king into legislating for a pogrom against the Jews in the Persian kingdom. He also planned to impale or hang Mordecai on a high gallows.

The story is complex, and filled with intrigue, but eventually we reach the denouement, reproduced at the beginning of this chapter. Mordecai has pleaded with Esther to save their people. She approaches the king, and both he and Haman are invited for meals with Esther. She reveals her ethnicity and the fact that one man is responsible for the imperilment of her people's lives. She identifies the man as Haman. The king is outraged. His judgement is swift.

With poetic justice Haman is impaled on the very pole he had set up for Mordecai.

The story has not one but several happy endings!

- Although the king's original edict for the annihilation of the Jews cannot be withdrawn, they are given the right to defend themselves (which they successfully do)
- Xerxes gives Esther Haman's estate
- Mordecai is promoted to a position second in power only to the king
- The festival of Purim is instigated

The king ordered Haman's execution. Was this legal? Yes. The king of Persia was all-powerful in his domain. His word was law. He didn't need to go through any legal process in order to execute anybody.

Nevertheless, we might consider today what charge(s) could have been levelled against Haman. Undoubtedly he had murderous thoughts, and fully intended genocide. On the basis of the Scripture quoted at the beginning, it has also been suggested that the king suspected Haman of making advances towards Esther. The king was jealous of his consort. Others might admire her, and he would have been content, indeed pleased that this was so, but he accused Haman of molesting her! That could not pass unavenged. The king may have been wrong in his interpretation of Haman's actions at the time, but there can be but little doubt that the merest suspicion would have been sufficient to secure a fatal outcome for Haman in those days.

Purim is a Jewish holiday which celebrates Haman's death and Jewish survival as documented in the book of Esther. The word means 'lots', and refers to the lots thrown by Haman to determine the date for his pogrom against the Jews. It takes place in the synagogue in a carnival atmosphere with singing, the telling of jokes, and foot stamping. It is a joyous occasion. As Reid[59] comments:

---

[59] Debra Reid, *Esther*, TOTC (Downers Grove: IVP, 2008), p.151.

> The festival is thus a vivid reminder that unexpected reversals do happen in history, and such reversals have a permanent impact on the life of the community of faith who celebrate the powerful presence of God among them.

DISCUSSION

By now it will be obvious that jealousy is a Hydra, a many headed monster. It can present in a number of different ways. Not only that, its presentation can be the consequence of different combinations of circumstances. Because of this, it can present insidiously and without the affected individual being very aware of it, especially at the outset. Additionally, and importantly, its consequences can be far-reaching and of the most serious nature. It must thus never be ignored or treated as trivial.

Cain was jealous of his brother Abel and murdered him.

Joseph's brothers were jealous of the preferential treatment afforded to him, and also affronted at (as they would have seen it) the grandiose content of his dreams – he was going to be the big boss to whom they would have to be subservient. Although they did not proceed with their plans for his demise, this was at least in large part to the circumstances which pertained at the time.

David's sin resulted from his illicit sexual desire for, and consequent illicit sexual affair with, the wife of one of his senior officers. One might ask where jealousy rears its ugly head here. It may not have been the predominant emotion of David in his murderous intent, but one can certainly perceive its presence. David was jealous of Uriah because he was the husband of Bathsheba who David coveted. As has already been noted, sexual jealousy can be a very destructive emotion.

Jezebel's acts against Naboth were not principally the result of jealousy in herself, but rather jealousy on the part of her husband. He was behaving like a spoilt child because he couldn't get what he wanted – Naboth's vineyard. One might look on it as jealousy at one step removed. Nevertheless, it was his jealousy that underpinned her homicidal actions.

The situation in the story which features Esther is also not straightforward. It to involves a number of complex and intertwining emotions, jealousy being one. Haman is a detestable character, probably incorporating narcissistic and anti-social (psychopathic) traits. Into this noxious substrate we can add his hatred of the Jewish people (which may have had historical origins), and his resentment at the refusal of Mordecai (a Jew) to offer him obeisance. His sentiments are further inflamed by his jealousy at the honour afforded to Mordecai when he thought it was going to be directed towards his own person!

One of the features which can be noted here is that although jealousy is a common human emotion, its expression is influenced by the underlying personality traits. Jezebel could have told her husband to grow up and not sulk because his wishes had been thwarted. She, on the other hand, clearly had a well-developed sense of entitlement and position in life. No one was going to stand in the way of the royal family and its wishes, however wilful they might be. Naboth was the victim of her husband's jealousy, but she was the killer of Naboth.

We end this section with a reminder of our own responsibilities as delineated in the tenth commandment:

> You shall not covet your neighbour's house. You shall not covet your neighbour's wife or his male or female servant, his ox or donkey, or anything that belongs to your neighbour. (Exodus 20:17, cf. Deuteronomy 5:21)

Chapter Eight
REVENGE

Introduction

The act of revenge involves causing harm to someone as a punishment for harm they have caused someone else. Often this is referred to as 'getting your own back'. History and literature are replete with tales of this nature.

One might think of the young Julius Caesar who was captured by pirates when sailing in the Aegean Sea. He was ransomed and freed, but not before he had informed them that he would capture them and crucify them. After his release he did just that. One Central Asian empire killed trade emissaries sent by Genghis Khan. He obliterated it.

'The Count of Monte Cristo' is a well-known novel by Alexandre Dumas. In it, the principal character, Edmond Dantes is wrongfully imprisoned, thus losing his promising future and his wife-to-be. Many years later he escapes, becomes exceedingly rich, and takes revenge on those responsible for his incarceration. Charles Dickens also uses the theme of revenge in 'Great Expectations'. Miss Havisham is a wealthy spinster who had been stood up at the altar decades previously by her husband-to-be. She continued to wear her wedding gown and became progressively more bitter about her plight. She also raised Estella, her adopted daughter, but planned to use her as a weapon of revenge against the cruelty of the male sex.

Most people can think of wrongs done to them during their lives, some minor, and some not so. Many will have contemplated acts of revenge, again some minor and some not. Most will have resigned themselves to idle contemplation rather than translating their thoughts into action. Some will have done so because of fear of the consequences of their fantasised ideation. Many such thoughts are serious in their consequence, and often involve criminal activity. Christians will be guided by the precepts of Scripture, as will be discussed in the discussion segment for this section of the book.

What is clear is that what at first sight might appear a simple concept of cause and effect is in fact complex. Both the range of precipitating factors, and the nature and consequences of the subsequent responses are extremely wide-ranging. As always, the personality of the individuals concerned are of great significance. Without wishing to use technical concepts and language, it can be readily appreciated that some individuals are more liable to recognise perceived slights and take them to heart. Their personality traits also mediate their responses to these. Someone who is prone to aggression may respond with violence. Others of a more reflective disposition may revert to a more subtle, calculated, but not necessarily less damaging response. An impulsive individual is prone to act off the cuff, so to speak, whereas others of a contrasting personality profile may bide their wrath, sometimes for years, before striking.

Given the very wide range of factors, and their complex interaction, one would expect to see very diverse scenarios as they play out, and so we do, in history, in literature, in everyday life, and indeed, in the pages of Scripture.

The instances from the Bible referred to in this chapter cover a lengthy period of time and encompass a variety of cultural backgrounds and historical situations. From a hermeneutical (Bible interpretation) perspective, I would encourage readers to look at the personality features, either made explicit, or inferred, in the biblical text. As a general principle, this is a worthwhile exercise, and often ignored or skimmed over. These are real people, and their character traits and emotions are often important in appreciating the theological import of the text.

LAMECH

GENESIS 4:17-24

> Cain made love to his wife, and she became pregnant and gave birth to Enoch. Cain was then building a city, and he named it after his son Enoch. To Enoch was born Irad, and Irad was the father of Mehujael, and Mehujael was the father of Methushael, and Methushael was the father of Lamech.
>
> Lamech married two women, one named Adah and the other Zillah. Adah gave birth to Jabal; he was the father of those who live in tents and raise livestock. His brother's name was Jubal; he was the father of all who play stringed instruments and pipes. Zillah also had a son, Tubal-Cain, who forged all kinds of tools out of bronze and iron. Tubal-Cain's sister was Naamah.
>
> Lamech said to his wives,
>
> 'Adah and Zillah, listen to me;
> wives of Lamech, hear my words.
> I have killed a man for wounding me.
> A young man for injuring me.
> If Cain is avenged seven times,
> Then Lamech seventy-seven times.'

Traditionally, as Hughes[60] reminds us, Lamech's poem has been called 'The Song of the Sword', and this ascription (if accurate), requires but little explanation other than perhaps to note that by now, the forging skills developed by Tubal-Cain may have been directed towards the fashioning of weapons.

Here, we are in very early times. Adam and Eve have been evicted from Eden, and their son Cain has killed his brother Abel. A third son, Seth, has yet to be born. Lamech, as can be seen, is from the line

---

[60] R. Kent Hughes, *Genesis: Beginning & Blessing*, PTW (Wheaton: Crossway, 2004), p.113.

of Cain. We read that Lamech says to his two wives that he has killed a man who injured him.

The chronological context of Lamech is the period between the fall and the flood. If we assume that his mindset is typical of his peers (although recognising that this cannot necessarily be assumed), it is not difficult to see how with successive generations to follow him, that the human condition could have become debased to the extent where 'The Lord regretted that he had made human beings on the earth, and his heart was deeply troubled' (Genesis 6:6).

When I read the above passage of Scripture, as well as reading it from a theological point of view, I also read it as a forensic psychiatrist, regarding it as part of the witness statement bundle which would accompany instructions from either the prosecution or defence to prepare a court report in a murder case.

One of the first things to leap off the page would be the necessity to carefully explore the personality characteristics in this case. Something of Lamech's character is evident in his poetic words. He is clearly boastful. He is very confident in his own abilities. He has killed another human being for injuring him. His hyperbolic statement regarding the degree of his vengeance is concerning. There is no further factual information, but further possibilities might reasonably be inferred. He certainly appears to be egotistical with narcissistic and impulsive traits. Nevertheless, these observations are not part of a court report, and it is not possible to clarify them further.

Essentially the question here, from the point of view of legal proceedings today, would be whether Lamech, if facing a charge of murder, would be considered as suffering from an abnormality of mind as to substantially impair his responsibility for his acts or omissions. My first thought would be to substantiate or exclude the diagnosis of psychopathic disorder, which equates (approximately) with the more recent diagnostic categorisation of dissocial personality disorder in ICDS-10. For those readers of a more technical disposition, I would refer them back to the diagnostic criteria already provided on page 111.

Obviously, the above classificatory detail is appropriate to our own time and culture and cannot of necessity be translated wholesale into that of Lamech. Nevertheless, I include it so the reader can compare it with that which is known of Lamech from the biblical record (which I would emphasise is insufficient for formal diagnostic purposes).

In non-technical language, one might expect him to be an overbearing character with thinly concealed aggression, full of himself and his own opinions which would be expressed in loud and authoritative terms. Very likely, his wives would have been afraid of him, and domestic marital violence would be no surprise.

The details of the violent incident are not divulged. It would certainly appear on the surface at least that Lamech's actions followed an attack on him by the deceased. Likewise, the deceased appears to have been younger than him, although this in itself does not necessarily imply lesser physical ability. We don't know what precipitated the other party to attack Lamech. It is not impossible that it was the result of provocation by Lamech himself, although it is admittedly unwise to over-speculate.

Would Lamech have been charged with an offence today? On the basis of the available evidence, which is admittedly sparse, it is not possible to say with any confidence. Much hinges on the reason for the initial attack on him, its motivation, severity, and whether a weapon was used etcetera. It would also be necessary to ascertain the circumstances of Lamech's response, and whether or not he used a weapon.

In the event of Lamech being charged with an offence, if the above circumstances occurred today, in the event of him walking out of court post-trial with no conviction recorded against him, his bragging would doubtless know no bounds!

TAMAR

Genesis 38:24-26

> About three months later Judah was told, 'Your daughter-in-law Tamar is guilty of prostitution, and as a result she is now pregnant.'

> Judah said, 'Bring her out and let her be burned to death!'
>
> As she was being brought out, she sent a message to her father-in-law. 'I am pregnant by the man who owns these,' she said. And she added, 'See if you recognise whose seal and cord and staff these are.'
>
> Judah recognised them and said, 'She is more righteous than I, since I wouldn't give her to my son Shelah.' And he did not sleep with her again.

In order to understand this incident properly it is necessary to read the whole of Genesis 38, and also to have some familiarity with the concept of levirate marriage.

The principles of levirate marriage are outlined in Deuteronomy 25:5-10. The word is derived from the Latin word *levir* which refers to a husband's brother. Essentially, when a married man died childless, his brother was to take his wife in marriage, and, crucially, the children of this marriage were considered as children of the first husband. The first-born son would become the heir of the first husband.

Here, Judah, one of the sons of Jacob by Leah, moves away from his family and marries a Canaanite wife. There are three sons from this union, Er, Onan, and Shelah. Judah arranges the marriage of Er to Tamar. The Bible tells us that 'Er, Judah's firstborn, was wicked in the Lord's sight; so the Lord put him to death' (Genesis 38:7). The next in line, Onan then marries his deceased brother's widow, in line with the levirate principle. He has a vested interest in not producing a son who will be ascribed to his brother as this would mean he would no longer be Onan's heir. He avoids the possibility by practicing *coitus interruptus* when engaging in sexual relations with Tamar. 'What he did was wicked in the Lord's sight; so the Lord put him to death also' (Genesis 38:10).

Judah was concerned about the safety of his remaining son Shelah. We might speculate on what he might have thought Tamar might have had to do with the death of his first two sons. Perhaps not in terms of direct involvement in their deaths, but he might have wondered if she brought them bad luck or some similar concept. He sends her to live in her father's house, he says, until Shelah grows up. In actuality he has no intention of his third son marrying Tamar and potentially sharing the fate of the first two.

Some considerable time later, Judah's wife dies, and he has a period of mourning for her before resuming normal life. He travels with a friend, Hiram the Adullamite to nearby Timnah, where his sheep are being sheared.

Meanwhile, Tamar is informed of her father-in-law's journey. She discards her mourning clothes and dons a veil to conceal her identity. She goes to a spot on the road to Timnah and waits. Judah sees her and mistakes her for a prostitute. Judah propositions her and they negotiate terms. He offers to send her a young goat. Although Tamar is receptive to this suggestion, she balks at giving credit! How can she be sure in these circumstances that the debt will be honoured? She asks for a pledge as security, suggesting Judah's seal with its cord, and his staff. Although these items mean little in terms of their significance to us today, at that time they constituted proof of identity. This is a crucial point. In today's terms she was asking him for his passport and driving licence. The terms agreed, they have sexual relations. Afterwards, Tamar returns home where she again dons her widow's clothes.

Judah, true to his word, sends a goat by way of Hirah to the place of the tryst, but there is no prostitute to be found, and enquiries reveal that there had never been a prostitute plying her trade there. Judah decides to let the matter drop. He doesn't want it to become known that he has been duped by a prostitute.

Events now take a dramatic turn. Three months later Judah is told not only that Tamar is a prostitute, but that she is pregnant, as documented in the biblical passage at the beginning of this chapter. Judah's immediate response is to order her death by burning. This is a most unusual form of execution in the Old Testament, although prescribed for a man marrying his mother-in-law (Leviticus 20:14), and promiscuity by the daughter of a priest (Leviticus. 21:9).

Another dramatic turn! As Tamar is being led to the place of her execution she sends a message to Judah along with the pledge items, stating she is pregnant by the owner of the items. Judah is cut to the core and confesses, 'She is more righteous than I, since I wouldn't give her to my son Shelah' (Genesis 38:26). He did not have sexual relations with her again.

Judah recognised that Tamar had been true to the concept of levirate marriage whereas he had traduced it. As Mathews[61] points out, that Judah did not have sexual relations with her again indicates repentance on his part.

Nevertheless, there is a happy ending to this sorry tale! Tamar gave birth to twin boys, Perez and Zerah. Perez was part of the Messianic line, and he is named in the genealogy of Jesus in Matthew 1:3 (in which even Tamar is mentioned!)

Admittedly, it may be thought to be stretching matters to include this pericope under the section of this book dealing with revenge (the act of hurting or harming someone in return for an injury or wrong suffered at their hands). In thinking in this way, we are viewing matters from Judah's perspective. Look instead through the eyes of Tamar. Such motivation can be potentially be discerned here, not necessarily at the fully conscious level. She would undoubtedly have had maternal aspirations, indeed, the bearing of children in order to perpetuate the family name was a primary function of women in those days. Childlessness was viewed as a curse (1 Samuel 1), whereas to have many children was considered an indication of divine approbation (Genesis 16:10; 17:2, 20; Psalms 128:3). By refusing to sanction marriage between Tamar and his remaining son Shelah, Judah had wronged her. She wanted a child. She would get her own back on him by having *his* child!

Judah undoubtedly ordered Tamar's death. He clearly intended her demise. In legal terms Judah did not order her murder. Tamar had clearly engaged in sexual activity outside of a marital relationship, and the penalty was death.

One can readily appreciate that in all this, Judah is far from free of blame. He had thwarted the levirate law by sending Tamar away and

---

[61] Kenneth A. Mathews, *Genesis 11:27-50:26*, NAC (Nashville: B&H, 2005), p.723.

preventing her marriage with Shelah when he came of age. He had illicit sex with someone who he thought to be a prostitute, and then ordered the burning of a supposed prostitute! Nevertheless, when faced with the facts, as Mathews notes, he saw the situation for what it was and repented.

SIMEON AND LEVI

Genesis 34:1-4

> Now Dinah, the daughter Leah had borne to Jacob, went out to visit the women of the land. When Shechem son of Hamor the Hivite, the ruler of that area, saw her, he took her and raped her. His heart was drawn to Dinah daughter of Jacob; he loved the young woman and spoke tenderly to her. And Shechem said to his father Hamor, 'Get me this girl as my wife.'

Genesis 34:24-29

> All the men who went out of the city gate agreed with Hamor and his son Shechem, and every male in the city was circumcised.
>
> Three days later, while all of them were still in pain, two of Jacob's sons, Simeon and Levi, Dinah's brothers, took their swords and attacked the unsuspecting city, killing every male. They put Hamor and his son Shechem to the sword and took Dinah from Shechem's house and left. The sons of Jacob came upon the dead bodies and looted the city where their sister had been defiled. They seized their flocks and herds and donkeys and everything else of theirs in the city and out in the fields. They carried off all their wealth and all their women and children, taking as plunder everything in the houses.

This event takes place during the lifetime of the patriarch Jacob. Briefly, following his twin brother Esau's homicidal thoughts towards him following their father Isaac's bestowal of the blessing on Jacob rather than on Esau through the deceptive acts of both Jacob and his mother Rebekah, Jacob decamps from the family home to that of Laban, his mother's brother. On his journey there he has a dream at Bethel where he sees angels ascending and descending a stairway, and the Lord at its top. God reaffirms the three provisions of the Abrahamic covenant: the land of Canaan, innumerable descendants, and blessing to all the families of the earth through them (Genesis 28). When Jacob arrives at Haran, he meets, falls in love with, and marries Rachel, Laban's daughter. However Laban is a devious character and by subterfuge engineers his unwitting wedding to her older sister, Leah, first. Jacob has to work for Laban for seven years for the privilege of marrying each daughter. Laban's tricking Jacob into marrying his first (and probably unattractive) daughter extends to exploitation of Jacob's work, and with the connivance of his wives, he absconds with them and his (legitimately owned) livestock. Laban chases after him, catches up with him, whereupon occurs the well-known story of Rachel concealing Laban's household gods. Laban and Jacob come to an agreement and go their separate ways in peace. On his homeward journey Jacob is acutely aware of the unresolved enmity between him and his brother Esau. Nevertheless, this too is resolved (Genesis 32-34).

Eventually, Jacob arrives at the city of Shechem in Canaan and establishes his camp nearby. He buys land there and erects an altar which he names El Elohe Israel. It means: 'El is the God of Israel', or 'God, the God of Israel', or 'mighty is the God of Israel'. It is at this point that problems arise.

Jacob and Leah have one named daughter, Dinah (Genesis 30:21). She goes to visit some females in the city, is seen by the city ruler's son, who has sexual intercourse with her. The NIV uses the word 'raped' in relation to this act, and it appears likely that this is the intended meaning, but it *could* be interpreted as a consensual act. Nevertheless, the Hebrew certainly indicates a very negative action. Wenham[62] comments:

> "Laid her" instead of the more usual "lay with her" implies forcible illegitimate intercourse. "Shamed her" is another term always used to describe intercourse without marriage (e.g. Deuteronomy 21:14;22:29; 2

[62] Gordon Wenham, *Genesis 16-20*, WBC (Nashville: Nelson, 2000), p.311.

> Samuel 13:12). The duplication of very negative terms shows the author's strong disapproval of Schechem's behaviour.

Despite this, it is clear that Shechem (the ruler's son) is strongly attracted to Dinah as he subsequently entreats his father to negotiate his marriage to her. This he does, but in the interim Jacob's sons have returned from their work in the fields and are 'shocked and furious' (v.5) by the turn of events. Their reaction would doubtless have been precipitated by the fact that forced intercourse or intercourse without a proper marriage agreement was wholly unacceptable. Jacob's own thoughts on all of this are unrecorded.

Hamor proposes to Jacob the marriage of their respective children. Indeed, he offers an unlimited bride price and gift. Jacob's sons, (here probably Simeon and Levi are in mind), insist that their sister cannot be married to an uncircumcised male. At this point we need to remember the words of the Covenant of Circumcision which God made with Abraham in Genesis 17. Not only were male members of the Israelite community to be circumcised, but also those in the household 'who are not your offspring' (v.12). The brothers are faultless in their covenant knowledge! Shechem must be circumcised. Looking again at Hamor's words to Jacob in verse 8, it is readily apparent that he is proposing much more than a single marriage between his son and Dinah. He is suggesting amalgamation between his people and those of Jacob:

> Intermarry with us; give us your daughters and take our daughters for yourselves. You can settle among us; the land is open to you. Live in it, trade in it, and acquire property in it. (Genesis 34:9-10).

Were this to happen, not only Shechem, but the other males of the city would also have to be circumcised. The brothers agree to Shechem's proposal on this basis; otherwise there is no deal. The people of the city are unanimous in their approval, and all the males in the city are circumcised. So far, so good.

Circumcision of adult males is painful and debilitating for several days following the surgery. Three days later, when the males of the city were still in pain, and thus with limited ability to defend themselves, two of the brothers, Simeon and Levi, go into the city with their swords and kill every single male. When they so act, they take Dinah from Shechem's house. Significantly, she has not returned home after her encounter with Shechem.

There can be no doubt but that Simeon and Levi committed premeditated cold-blooded murder. Doubtless they were understandably incensed at the defilement of their sister Dinah. This likely would have been further accentuated by the fact that they shared the same mother (Leah) with Dinah and were thus full brothers. Their plan was formulated in advance of their homicidal acts. It was indeed a cunning scheme. The proposal for circumcision was based on divine command and would thus attract the approval of their father Jacob and others. It would be unlikely to engender suspicion in the inhabitants of the city who, doubtless, would have been informed of its provenance. The attack itself would have been completely unexpected, with the victims incapacitated to one extent or another. No wonder it worked!

It is always necessary to address motive, and here there is but little doubt. Simeon and Levi were determined to exact revenge against Shechem *and* his people for the deflowering of their sister. One needs to consider what led them to extend their vengeance beyond Shechem himself. A number of possibilities exist here, not all of them mutually exclusive. Their antagonism towards Shechem probably extended to his people as well, not just because they were related to him. Also, of very significant importance at that time, they would undoubtedly have been concerned about retribution were Shechem only to die. He was an important man in his community. His father was the ruler of the city. It is scarcely credible that his community would not have sought retribution for the life of their ruler's son. The killing of all the males in the city can therefore be seen as an entirely logical act, however distasteful it may seem to modern eyes. It will be left to the reader to decide whether the actions taken by Simeon and Levi were proportionate to the offence caused.

In today's world there can be no doubt that Simeon and Levi would have been charged with multiple counts of murder. There are no obvious grounds for the defence to attempt to secure convictions on the lesser charge of manslaughter. Their actions were clearly pre-planned and deliberate. There is not the slightest evidence that either suffered from any abnormality of mind which would have diminished their responsibility for their actions. Quite the reverse – it was a carefully conceived and executed plan.

MOSES

Exodus 2:11-15)

> One day, after Moses had grown up, he went out to where his own people were and watched them at their hard labour. He saw an Egyptian beating a Hebrew, one of his own people. Looking this way and that and seeing no one, he killed the Egyptian and hid him in the sand. The next day he went out and saw two Hebrews fighting. He asked the one in the wrong, 'Why are you hitting your fellow Hebrew?'
>
> The man said, 'Who made you ruler and judge over us? Are you thinking of killing me as you killed the Egyptian?' Then Moses was afraid and thought, 'What I did must have become known.'
>
> When Pharaoh heard of this, he tried to kill Moses, but Moses fled from Pharaoh and went to live in Midian, where he sat down by a well.

At this early stage in his life there is but limited information about Moses. We know that he is a Hebrew, and from Exodus 2:1 and 6:19-20 that his parents were Levites, his father being Amram, and his mother Jochebed. Pharaoh, being concerned over the burgeoning numbers of the Israelites had ordered that all male offspring be thrown into the Nile river, but Moses' mother had concealed him in a waterproofed papyrus basket and hidden it in the reeds which grew along the Nile. Pharaoh's daughter discovered the baby. Moses' sister was providentially at hand and offered to procure the services of a Hebrew woman to nurse the baby, and when this suggestion was accepted, she went and fetched her mother. Thus Moses was weaned by his own mother! Moses was thus brought up in the royal household, despite his humble beginnings.

The episode in his life which concerns us here occurred after he had grown up in royal surroundings. He went out and saw the Hebrews at their toil. He was clearly aware of his background as those he watched are described as his own people.

Moses saw an Egyptian (presumably an overseer) beating a Hebrew male. After carefully checking that there were no witnesses, he killed the Egyptian and hid his body in the sand. The next day he went out again and this time saw two Hebrew men fighting, He asked one why he was striking a fellow countryman, and the man's rather sarcastic reply made it clear that his previous day's actions were known. He had been seen! When this became known to Pharaoh, he tried to kill Moses, but he was able to escape, and found refuge far away, out of Pharaoh's reach, in Midian.

That Moses killed the Egyptian overseer is not in question. One or more witnesses had clearly seen his actions, otherwise the Hebrew attacker the following day would not have been aware of it. There can be no doubt either that Moses knew he had done wrong. He had looked for anyone around who might have witnessed his actions before his attack on the Egyptian and had concealed his body afterwards. As a result, Pharaoh was planning to kill him, and Moses went on the run.

Knowledge of the Egyptian legal system of the time and its penalties for offences is far from complete. Additionally, legal systems are prone to change over time, and the actual dates for Moses' life are uncertain. If one looks at the proposed dates for the exodus, some scholars opt for an early date around 1446 BC, and others for a later date of around 1269 BC. Nonetheless, it seems likely that the penalty for murder was execution, and that this was indeed so tends to be confirmed by Pharaoh's intention to kill Moses once he had learned of the incident.

Ryken[63] comments:

> Moses was never brought to trial, but if he had been, it might not have been hard to defend him. For starters, what he did was not premeditated; it was merely a crime

[63] Philip Graham Ryken, *Exodus*, PTW (Wheaton: Crossway, 2005), p.57.

> of passion, if indeed it was a crime at all. Furthermore, from the standpoint of Egyptian law, Moses probably was within his rights. As a prince of Egypt he held the power of the sword, and it is doubtful whether a member of Pharaoh's court would have been condemned simply for killing a slave driver. The Hebrew verdict on Moses would have been even more favorable, for as far as the Israelites were concerned, Moses was a patriot.

I am aware that many Christian commentators, including Tertullian and Aquinas have tried to find Moses not guilty of murder in this particular matter, but it is difficult to accept Ryken's comments at face value. The attack *was* premeditated. That much is clear from Moses looking around for witnesses prior to then attacking the Egyptian. I am unclear as to his use of the words 'merely a crime of passion'. Such a concept may exist in law on the European continent in an entirely different context but is unknown in UK law or in Doctor Ryken's native America. His query as to whether this can be considered a crime at all is similarly incomprehensible. A human being was killed following an intentional attack by another human being.

Would Moses have faced a charge of murder in today's society? Almost certainly. Whether or not he would be found guilty would be a matter for deliberation by the jury after they had heard all the evidence during the proceedings of the court.

Presumably there would be no claim that Moses was not responsible for the man's death. The defence would likely seek a conviction for manslaughter rather than murder. All murder charge cases are examined pre-trial by at least one psychiatrist for the prosecution and almost always at least one for the defence. The reason for this is to determine whether there could be grounds for a finding of manslaughter on the basis of diminished mental responsibility. Without going into technical detail this essentially means: did the accused suffer from a mental disorder, and if so, did it substantially diminish his responsibility for his actions? This is a simple way of looking at the issue, but arguably sufficient for our purposes here.

On the basis of the available evidence, pleading not guilty to murder, but guilty to manslaughter on the basis of diminished responsibility would not be open to the defence. There has been no hint of mental disorder in relation to Moses (and neither is this the case in relation to his later life).

The possible partial defence to murder (and if successful, resulting in a conviction for manslaughter) on the basis of loss of self -control might be employed in Moses' case. Moses would have had to have acted here in justified anger. The sort of case where such a defence might be successful is where the defendant discovers the deceased abusing his child, flies into a rage, and kills him. Whether a jury would find in this way for Moses is debatable. Juries do sometimes return with unexpected verdicts. Either way, Moses would still have a conviction for causing the death of another human being. It is to my mind almost inconceivable that in a court today he would not be convicted of either murder or manslaughter.

Christians rightly have a high regard for Moses (as do those of the Jewish faith). He was mightily used by God. He was called by God, negotiated the exit of the Israelites from Egypt, received the law at Mount Sinai, and led them for forty difficult years through the desert, to the borders of the promised land. It is easy to remember Moses with rose coloured spectacles just in terms of his close relationship with God and his many achievements. Nonetheless, this is not to have a well-rounded picture of his character. Even after being called by God, as with other prominent biblical figures, he had his failings.

In Numbers 20:8-13 we encounter an episode where Moses does not follow God's instructions. The Israelites are again complaining about lack of water. Moses receives God's instructions to speak to the rock in order to obtain water. Instead of speaking to it, he strikes it. Although God graciously provides water, Moses (and Aaron) were punished by not being allowed to lead the people into the promised land. Various reasons have been offered for this judgement by God, but Coakley's[64] is the one preferred here:

> The stated reason in the text is not due to their disobedience but their lack of faith ('because you have not believed Me, to treat Me as holy in the sight of the

[64] James Coakley, in *The Moody Bible Commentary*, ed. Michael Rydelnik and Michael Vanlaningham (Chicago: Moody, 2014), p.243.

> sons of Israel, v.12). The form of the verb "believe" here involves acknowledging what someone says as true, but it also has the added meaning of acting in response to what is heard with trust or obedience.
>
> The Lord stressed that their unbelief led to the people's premature death in the wilderness. Their sin was wholly a lack of faith and trust in the Lord. Certainly Moses, Aaron, and the Israelites disobeyed the Lord, but that was the fruit of their unbelief, not the root cause of their punishment. It was not a failure to keep the law that led to their death in the wilderness. Instead, just as the people had failed to believe God and trust Him in chapter 14, so also Moses and Aaron were lacking in faith.

It is often emphasised that Moses' actions against the Egyptian overseer occurred prior to his calling by God in Exodus 3. That is indeed so, but does not in itself in any way exculpate him from his actions. Moses was a killer, and in today's legal system may well have been found guilty of murder.

One thing can be learned from this sorry episode. Moses still identified with the Hebrew nation despite being reared in the Egyptian court. He was clearly incensed by the exploitation of his people including the callous way in which they could be treated by their Egyptian masters. He felt impelled to act on their behalf. Although we should not of course emulate Moses in the extent to which he pursued his outrage, we should note that he did not stand idly by whilst vulnerable others were mistreated. There are plenty of examples of people being taken advantage of in today's world. Christians, as well as recognising this, should not stand idly by either.

GIDEON

Judges 8:18-21

> Then he asked Zebah and Zalmunna, 'What kind of men did you kill at Tabor?' 'Men like you,' they answered, 'each one with the bearing of a prince.' Gideon replied, 'Those were my brothers, the sons of my own mother.

> As surely as the Lord lives, if you had spared their lives, I would not kill you. Turning to Jether, his eldest son, he said, 'Kill them!' But Jether did not draw his sword, because he was only a boy and was afraid. Sebah and Zalminna said, 'Come, do it yourself. "As is the man, so is his strength."' 'So Gideon stepped forward and killed them, and took the ornaments off their camels' necks.

We need to put this passage in its context to better understand it.

Gideon has routed the Midianite army by his night-time attack using only 300 troops with trumpets, pitchers, and torches. As McMath[65] points out, the trumpets would have been *shofars*, an instrument made from ram's horns. Usually only the leader of a military unit would have access to one of these, so the blowing of 300 of them might well have suggested a huge army to the Midianite troops. The torches, on the other hand, might well have impressed the Midianites as the campfires of a great army. Thus, it was possible for a mere 300 of Gideon's men to put the Midianites to flight.

Other Israelite tribes were called on to pursue the fleeing Midianites, and two of the enemy leaders, Oreb and Zeeb were killed by men of Ephraim. Meanwhile, Gideon and his 300 men pursue the two Midianite kings who controlled the enemy forces. The kings are captured. Now we come to the biblical passage reproduced above. Gideon then asks what might impress as an unusual question. He enquires as to what sort of men they had killed at Tabor. The victims are then identified as Gideon's brothers. Israelite extended families could have numerous children, particularly as the head of the family might have several wives/concubines. Here, as Gideon points out, as the victims were 'my brothers, the sons of my own mother', they had a particular consanguinity (blood relationship) to Gideon. They were his full brothers, and thus merited especial affection and loyalty. Gideon tells the two kings that if they had spared his brothers, he would have spared them. They had not, and thus Gideon kills them.

There are a number of legal issues here, and they are different, depending on whether we are looking at them as if they were reported

---

[65] John McMath, in *The Moody Bible Commentary*, ed. Michael Ryderlnik and Michael Vanlaningham (Chicago: Moody, 2014), p.373.

in yesterday's newspaper (as we often read Scripture!), or if we look on them in terms of the cultural norms of that time.

The two kings had been captured during hostilities, and thus in today's terms would be considered as prisoners of war. They would thus be subject to the Geneva Convention and protected from summary execution. No such convention existed at that time, nor until comparatively recently. Throughout most of history, captured enemy troops have been subject to the death sentence, or at least a subsequent life of misery. The Romans, for example, would not necessarily kill enemy soldiers captured in battle, but as an alternative would trade them (and their families) to those whose business was dealing in slaves. This was an attractive option, not for humanitarian reasons, but because the troops would share in the money resulting from the sale!

Gideon, in his time, probably had in mind a factor which is not immediately obvious to us today, as pointed out by Stone.[66] Gideon's brothers had been killed by Zebah and Zalmunna. Under the provisions of Numbers 35:9-34, they had been deliberately killed, and under these circumstances 'that person is a murderer; the murderer is to be put to death' (Numbers 35:16). The Numbers passage goes on to say, ''The avenger of blood shall put the murderer to death; when the avenger comes upon the murderer, the avenger shall put the murderer to death' (Numbers 35:19).

Gideon's brothers had been murdered. He had an obligation under the law as the 'avenger of blood'. He waited until victory had been secured for his people before pursuing his obligation.

Justice was done!

ABIMELEK

Judges 9:1- 6

> Abimelek son of Jerub-Baal went to his brother's brothers in Shechem and said to them and to all his

[66] Lawson G. Stone, *Joshua, Judges, Ruth*, Cornerstone (Carol Stream: Tyndale, 2012), p.294-295.

> mother's clan, 'Ask all the citizens of Shechem, "Which is better for you: to have all seventy of Jerub-Baal's sons rule over you, or just one man?" Remember, I am your flesh and blood.'
>
> When the brothers repeated all this to the citizens of Shechem, they were inclined to follow Abimelek, for they said, 'He is related to us.' They gave him seventy shekels of silver from the temple of Baal-Berith, and Abimelek used it to hire reckless scoundrels, who became his followers. He went to his father's home in Ophrah and on one stone murdered his seventy brothers, the sons of Jerub-Baal. But Jotham, the youngest son of Jerub-Baal, escaped by hiding. Then all the citizens of Shechem and Beth Millo gathered beside the great tree at the pillar in Shechem to crown Abimelek king.

Jerub-Baal is better known to most as the well-known Old Testament character Gideon. It will be recalled that in Judges 6:25-32 Gideon, in response to God's command, destroyed his father's altar to Baal, and built an altar to Yahweh the one true God. Verse 32 tells us that the people subsequently gave him a new name: 'So because Gideon broke down Baal's altar, they gave him the name Jerub-Baal that day, saying, "Let Baal contend with him."' The name can also be translated, 'let Baal make his case'. Yahweh, not Baal, is the God of Gideon. He has, as it were, nailed his colours to the mast, in the midst of pagan, or at best, syncretistic worship. Gideon is arguably best remembered for his stunning victory over the Midianites with three hundred men, trumpets, and jars. Our interest here, however, is not primarily in Gideon and his notable life, but with his family.

Abimelek was Gideon's son by a Shechemite concubine. There were seventy other sons. We have but little by way of knowledge of his early life but can draw some inferences. He appears to have had but little if any empathy for his brothers, and this may reflect his upbringing. That it is recorded in verse 1 that he went to Shechem to visit his mother's brothers might suggest that he had been living at his father's residence rather than with his mother, and if so, he might have been separated from his mother at a young age. We might also wonder whether the other brothers were born to Israelite women, whilst Abimelek's mother was clearly of a different ethnic origin –

she was Canaanite, and thus outside of the covenant people. Thus, when growing up he may have been made to feel inferior because of his mother's status (or lack of it), and he likely felt himself an outsider in the family household. This could have engendered simmering resentment and a desire to get back on those he perceived as his tormentors. This, admittedly, is speculation, but it would fit with the facts as we know them.

At the start of Judges 9, it is clear that Abimelek has formulated a plan. He goes to Shechem and approaches close members of his mother's family (her brothers), and also her extended family (his mother's clan). He tells them to enquire of all the inhabitants of Shechem whether it would be better for them to be ruled by Gideon's seventy sons, or by him. He then reminds them of his biological ties to them. It sounds as though Abimelek is running for election, and so he is!

His campaign message is accepted by the citizens who are impressed by his blood relationship to them (Gideon's sons are of different ethnicity). They contribute to his campaign coffers to the tune of seventy shekels of silver (about 1.75 pounds). Interestingly, this is liberated from the temple of Baal-Berith. One immediately has a hint as to how this tale is going to end. We have God's covenant people on the one hand, and Canaanite opposition financed by the temple of a pagan god on the other! Abimelek uses the windfall to hire 'reckless scoundrels', a term which Lawson Younger[67] informs us can literally be translated, 'men empty and audaciously reckless'. We get the picture!

Abimelek now takes his band of hired ruffians to his father's home at Ophrah and kills sixty-nine of Gideon's sons. The description of the killing of the sons suggests it was conducted in a serial manner, one son being dispatched after the other. The sole surviving son later publicly tells a fable which essentially constitutes a curse, which is to be found in verses 7-15.

There can be no doubt that these killings constituted acts of premeditated murder.

---

[67] K. Lawson Younger Jr., *Judges/Ruth*, NIVAC (Grand Rapids: Zondervan, 2002), p.221.

There are probably two main motives here, albeit intertwined. The first is revenge against his family. He all but certainly resented the way other members of the household treated him, and his ethnic background would likely have contributed towards this. He was not part of the 'proper' family grouping. Today this would probably be regarded as an example of racial prejudice. Second, rather than feeling like a second-class citizen, he wanted to be in charge – to be the boss. Thus misconceived ambition would also have been a potent motivating factor.

There is also a possible other influential factor in operation, and that is Abimelech's personality. He is clearly an utterly ruthless individual. He has no semblance of any affection for his brothers, indeed quite the reverse. Indeed, one might wonder about his capacity for affection towards any other human being. His courting of his mother's family can be seen purely as a manipulative act designed to further his malign ambition.

At this point, I, as a forensic psychiatrist, would be seeking to exclude the possibility of a personality disorder. The issue of the classification of the personality disorders is too complex to explore here. As already noted, I don't think that the Bible gives us sufficient information to make a definitive diagnosis of this type in any biblical character, although in other individuals, such as Lamech, as with Abimelek, there are pointers. He presents as a thoroughly unpleasant, unfeeling, nasty individual. You wouldn't like Abimelek if you met him! The possibility of a psychopathic personality disorder (now known as an anti-social personality disorder) would necessitate exploration by the examining psychiatrist.

As already noted, in today's world, Abimelek would be facing multiple charges of murder. Although the evidence against him would likely be incontrovertible, this does not necessarily mean that he would enter a plea of guilty on all counts. His defence team would have commissioned at least one psychiatric report (as would the prosecution). In this instance the defence may be able to identify a psychiatrist who will give evidence that he suffers from a mental disorder (a disorder of personality) of a nature and degree that substantially impaired his responsibility at the material time. If the jury is swayed by this testimony, the result will be a verdict of manslaughter rather than murder. If the prosecution have contrasting expert evidence, this will be tested in court leading to what is known as 'contested diminished' proceedings.

If convicted of murder in the UK today, there is only one penalty the judge could impose, specifically that of life imprisonment. If he is convicted of manslaughter the judge's hands are said to be 'untied', and a wide range of sentencing powers are available to the judge, including non-custodial ones (that is, not being sentenced to prison). If he is found to be suffering from a mental disorder which merits medical care and treatment, there is likely to be a recommendation for hospital care and treatment. In view of the nature of this case, any such disposal by the court would be to a hospital providing maximum secure care and treatment. In England this would mean placement in Broadmoor, Rampton or Ashworth Hospitals.

Abimelek later comes to a violent end himself, as can be learned from Judges 9:22-56. God did not tolerate his killings (Judges 9:23-24, 56).

SAMSON

Judges 16:23-30

> Now the rulers of the Philistines assembled to offer a great sacrifice to Dagon their god and to celebrate, saying, 'Our god has delivered Samson, our enemy, into our hands.'
>
> When the people saw him, they praised their god, saying,
>
> > 'Our god has delivered our enemy into our hands,
> > the one who laid waste our land and multiplied our
> > slain.'
>
> While they were in high spirits, they shouted, 'Bring out Samson to entertain us.' So they called Samson out of the prison, and he performed for them.
>
> When they stood him among the pillars, Samson said to the servant who held his hand, 'put me where I can feel

> the pillars that support the temple so that I may lean against them.' Now the temple was crowded with men and women; all the rulers of the Philistines were there, and on the roof were about three thousand men and women watching Samson perform. Then Samson prayed to the Lord, 'Sovereign Lord, remember me. Please, God, strengthen me just once more, and let me with one blow get revenge on the Philistines for my two eyes.'
>
> Then Samson reached towards the two central pillars on which the temple stood. Bracing himself against them, his right hand on the one and his left hand on the other, Samson said, 'Let me die with the Philistines!' Then he pushed with all his might, and down came the temple on the rulers and all the people in it. Thus he killed many more when he died than while he lived.

Samson was born in Zorah, a town of the tribe of Dan, and it was close to land occupied by the Philistines. This geographical proximity is important, for we read early on in the biblical account of Samson that the angel of the Lord tells his mother: 'He will take the lead in delivering Israel from the hands of the Philistines' (Judges 13:5). His mother, prior to his conception, had been childless, a potent cause of shame in that culture. When this was declared to his mother-to-be, she was also told that he was to be raised as a Nazirite. This latter term merits explanation. Essentially it refers to consecration, devotion, and separation.[68] The Nazirite had to abstain from wine and other intoxicating drinks, not cut his hair, and have no contact with a dead body (Numbers 6:1-21). The period to which these restrictions applied was usually time limited. In the New Testament, it may be recalled, the Apostle Paul took a Nazirite vow for a fixed period of time (Acts 18:18; 21:22-26). Samson, on the other hand, was to be a life-long Nazirite.

But Samson was not a faithful Nazirite!

To the chagrin of his parents Samson tells them he wants to marry a Philistine woman. The Bible informs that 'His parents did not know that this was from the Lord, who was seeking an occasion to confront

---

[68] *Holman Illustrated Bible Dictionary* (Nashville: B&H, 2003), p.1178.

the Philistines; for at that time they were ruling over Israel' (Judges 14:4). Samson later kills a lion, and on coming across its dead carcass later, scoops out some honey that bees have left there, and eats it. It will be remembered here that contact with dead bodies is forbidden to Nazirites. There is then a wedding feast at which there would likely have been heavy drinking (again forbidden to Nazirites), and whilst there he has a very substantial bet with thirty Philistine men that they cannot solve the puzzle he sets for them. They then threaten the life of his wife if she does not reveal the answer to them. This she does. Samson has to honour his bet and provide clothing for thirty Philistines! He does so by going to Ashkelon (a Philistine city), killing thirty men, stripping them, and thus fulfilling his wager. He returns to his father's house in a furious mood.

Later, Samson goes to visit his wife only to find her father has given her to one of the other attendees at his wedding. He is determined on vengeance! He catches three hundred foxes, ties them in pairs by the tails, attaches a burning torch, and lets them loose in the ripening corn of the Philistines. Their corn, their vineyards, and their olive groves are destroyed! This would have been a catastrophic blow to the Philistines who would have relied for their food and livelihood on what they could grow.

This time round it is the Philistines who are out for revenge! The Philistines inveigle the Israelites to tie Samson up and hand him over to them. They do so, but Samson's strength breaks the bindings, he grabs the jawbone of a donkey, and kills a thousand of them.

One day Samson goes to Gaza, another Philistine city and spends the night with a prostitute. The Philistines, on learning of his presence, try to trap him, but Samson, utilising his great strength, takes away the city gates, and deposits them on a hill about thirty-seven miles away.

Now romance enters the story! Samson falls in love with Delilah. She is suborned by a large Philistine bribe, and after several unsuccessful attempts Samson is captured after he reveals to her that the secret of his immense strength lies in the length of his hair. She has it cut whilst he is sleeps on her lap. He is now vulnerable and is apprehended by the Philistines who gouge out his eyes and consign him to grinding their corn in prison.

We now arrive at the events related in the passage at the beginning of this chapter. The Philistines are offering a sacrifice, and celebrating to Dagon, their god for delivering Samson to them. Samson prays to God for strength to avenge his loss of sight, and pushes against the two central pillars which support the temple. The temple collapses, and all the people there, including Samson, are killed. Samson is revenged for the loss of his sight.

Looking at the climax of the Samson story through modern eyes, we might be inclined to look on it much as we do some terrorist atrocities. There is a religious context, and many people are killed by the unforeseen acts of one or more individuals. In this scenario, Samson would undoubtedly (had he survived) have been charged with murder, doubtless convicted, and in the UK, incarcerated.

But we can legitimately view these events from another perspective. Despite Samson's blatant disregard for his Nazirite vows, his disregard for the feelings of his parents, and his responsibilities to them under the Mosaic law (for example, the fifth commandment), his sexual infidelity etcetera, God was still working in his life. We have already seen this in Judges 14:4. We see it again in the final episode. As Hildebrand[69] puts it: 'The humiliated Samson called once again upon the Lord for assistance, and his vengeful motives again aligned with God's purpose of discomfiting the Philistines'. Despite his obvious imperfections, Samson was used by God in beginning the deliverance of Israel from the power of the Philistines.

Hebrews 11:32-33 provides a postscript to the Samson story. For all his deficiencies, he had faith in God. This is indicated by Judges 15:18 and 16:28. God's responses confirm the sincerity of his belief.

DOEG

1 Samuel 22:6-18

> Now Saul heard that David and his men had been discovered. And Saul was seated, spear in hand, under the tamarisk tree on the hill at Gibeah, with all his

---

[69] D. R, Hildebrand, *The International Standard Bible Encyclopedia*, Vol. 4, ed. Geoffrey W. Bromiley (Grand Rapids: Eerdmans, 1988), p.311.

officers standing at his side. He said to them, 'Listen, men of Benjamin! Will the son of Jesse give all of you fields and vineyards? Will he make all to you commanders of thousands and commanders of hundreds? Is that why you have all conspired against me? No one tells me when my son makes a covenant with the son of Jesse. None of you is concerned about me or tells me that my son has incited my servant to lie in wait for me, as he does today.'

But Doeg the Edomite, who was standing with Saul's officials, said, 'I saw the son of Jesse come to Ahimelek son of Ahitub at Nob. Ahimelek enquired of the Lord for him; he also gave him provisions and the sword of Goliath the Philistine.'

Then the king sent for the priest Ahimelek son of Ahitub and all the men of his family, who were the priests at Nob, and they all came to the king. Saul said, 'Listen now, son of Ahitub.'

"Yes, my lord,' he answered.

Saul said to him, 'Why have you conspired against me, you and the son of Jesse, giving him bread and a sword and enquiring of God for him, so that he has rebelled against me and lies in wait for me, as he does today?'

Ahimelek answered the king, 'Who of all your servants is as loyal as David, the king's son-in-law, captain of your bodyguard and highly respected in your household? Was that day the first time I enquired of God for him? Of course not! Let not the king accuse your servant or any of his father's family, for your servant knows nothing at all about this whole affair.'

But the king said, 'You shall surely die, Ahimelek, you and your whole family.'

Then the king ordered the guards at his side: 'Turn and kill the priests of the Lord, because they too have sided

> with David. They knew he was fleeing, yet they did not tell me.'
>
> But the king's officials were unwilling to raise a hand to strike the priests of the Lord.
>
> The king then ordered Doeg, 'You turn and strike down the priests.' So Doeg the Edomite turned and struck them down. That day he killed eighty-five men who wore the linen ephod. He also put to the sword Nob, the town of the priests, with its men and women, its children and infants, and its cattle, donkeys and sheep.

David is on the run! He has killed Goliath, married Saul's daughter Michal, and with her assistance has fled from Saul's determination to put him to death. Saul has already tried to kill David on more than one occasion. He was likely jealous of David and his military success, but crucially, he was afraid of him because he knew the Lord was with him (1 Samuel 18:12, 14, 28).

David goes to Nob, which appears to have been the main sanctuary location at that time. He lies to Ahimelek the priest there about his circumstances and demands food. The only bread available was consecrated bread, which had recently been removed from the special table designated for it and replaced with fresh bread. The priest, in view of David's obvious need, made an exception in giving him the bread. However, danger lurks. In 1 Samuel 21:7 we read, 'Now one of Saul's servants was there that day, detained before the Lord; he was Doeg the Edomite, Saul's chief shepherd.' Although the Edomites were descendants of Jacob, this was through Esau, and there had been a long history of enmity between the Israelites and the Edomites (Numbers 20:14-21; 24:18). The mention of Doeg thus introduces a sinister note to proceedings.

We now come to the passage quoted at the beginning of this chapter. Saul is sitting in the shade of a deciduous tree pointing out to his court officials (who like him are of the tribe of Benjamin), the advantages of affiliation to him rather than to David. It is clear from this that David is seen as a threat. Saul is concerned about the loyalty of his attendants. As I have previously documented,[70] I do not believe (as has been suggested), that Saul suffered at this time from a paranoid psychotic illness. I would regard his concerns as being wholly understandable, and normal in Saul's perception of his circumstances.

Doeg, standing in attendance, now sees his chance to ingratiate himself with the king. He tells him that David had approached the priest Ahimelek, who fed and armed him. He did not mention that David had lied to Ahimelek. Saul regarded Ahimelek's actions as treason. He summoned him and the other priests of his family. Ahimelek did not help his case when he defended David's actions, engendering more anger on the part of Saul who ordered his guards to kill the priests. The troops were too afraid to kill God's priests.

Saul orders Doeg to kill the priests. This he does, slaughtering eighty-five of them. He then kills all human and animal life in Nob.

It may be wondered why this episode is subsumed under the section of this book entitled 'revenge'. Essentially, Saul is avenging himself on David, albeit one step removed. Nevertheless, he is also taking revenge on Ahimelek, and his fellow priests, and their families for what Saul doubtless saw as consorting with and comforting his perceived enemy.

Doeg does the killing, but Saul gives the order. Saul's command is a regnal directive. Saul is king, his word is law, so what's the problem?

There is a big problem here. Saul is indubitably king, but Israel's kings were *not* autonomous. They were not in ultimate control. Israel was a theocracy. God ruled Israel. True, he had appointed Saul (and had already anointed David as king, although he had yet to take up the throne), but Saul was ultimately answerable to God. Additionally, he was subject to God's laws like the rest of the nation. This meant that he was subject to the provisions of the Decalogue (the Ten Commandments), and all the other legislation given to Moses at Mount Sinai. Saul had repeatedly disobeyed God. He had been

---

[70] Laurence J. Naismith, *Psychiatry, the Bible, and the Church* (Chichester: Faithbuilders, 2021), p.197-212.

unfaithful. His kingship years were drawing to an end and would finally be over with his ignominious death on Mount Gilboah (1 Samuel 31).

JOAB

2 Samuel 3:22-30

> Just then David's men and Joab returned from a raid and brought with them a great deal of plunder. But Abner was no longer with David in Hebron, because David had sent him away, and he had gone in peace. When Joab and all the soldiers with him arrived, he was told that Abner son of Ner had come to the king and that he had gone in peace.
>
> So Joab went to the king and said, 'What have you done? Look, Abner came to you. Why did you let him go? Now he is gone! You know Abner son of Ner; he came to deceive you and observe your movements and find out everything you are doing.'
>
> Joab then left David and sent messengers after Abner, and they brought him back from the cistern at Sirah. But David did not know it. Now when Abner returned to Hebron, Joab took him aside into an inner chamber, as if to speak with him privately. And there, to avenge the blood of his brother Asahel, Joab stabbed him in the stomach, and he died.
>
> Later, when David heard about this, he said, 'I and my kingdom are for ever innocent before the Lord concerning the blood of Abner son of Ner. May his blood fall on the head of Joab and on his whole family! May Joab's family never be without someone who has a running sore or leprosy or who leans on a crutch or who falls by the sword or who lacks food.'
>
> (Joab and his brother Abishai murdered Abner because he had killed their brother Asahel in the battle of Gibeon.)

The killing of Asahel by Abner is given as the motive for Joab and Abishai to take the life of their brother's killer. Their act was thus one of revenge. The story of Abner killing Asahel is contained elsewhere in this book, and thus only outline details of that event will be provided here.

The time period here follows the death of Saul. David is based in Hebron and is ruling over the southern part of the land, that is, Judah. The northern territory is essentially short of a formal leader. Nevertheless, Abner, who was Saul's military commander, is powerful, and after Saul's death, David enters into negotiations with him. Saul's son Ish-bosheth had been supported by Abner until Ish-bosheth accused him of sleeping with his father's concubine. Abner was furious at this and transferred his loyalty to David (2 Samuel 3:6-21). Abner had consulted the elders of Israel and essentially had made an agreement that David was to be king of the entire country, effectively bringing reconciliation between the north and the south, and uniting the land under one monarch once again. It was for this purpose that Abner had visited David, this event bringing us to the passage quoted above.

Joab was David's military commander during most of his reign. He was the oldest son of Zeruiah, the sister of David (2 Samuel. 2:13; 1 Chronicles 2:16) He was a ruthless character but had been effective in the capture of Jerusalem (1 Chronicles 11:4-8), and in the campaign against the Ammonites (2 Samuel 10). It is noted here that it was during the latter military action that David sent his shameful order to Joab, instructing him to engineer the death of Uriah, the husband of Bathsheba, during the fighting. He is also remembered as the individual who brokered reconciliation between David and Absalom (2 Samuel 14). The relationship had fractured following Absalom's killing of his half-brother Amnon after the latter had raped his (Absalom's) full sister. Thus Joab had been a valued and trusted member of David's entourage, with his loyalty unswerving, at least until the time when David was coming to the end of his life, when he supported Adonijah's claim to the throne (1 Kings 1:17-19), but that is another story.

Abishai was also a son of Zeruiah and thus Joab's younger brother (1 Samuel 26:6). He is mentioned elsewhere in the Old Testament a number of times, but notably he was with David on one of the occasions where he spared Saul (1 Samuel 26:7).

Joab in particular was incensed by the death of his brother Asahel and clearly had a thirst for vengeance against Abner. This was clearly shared by his brother Abishai as they jointly murdered Abner.

Joab and his fellow raiders arrive back at David's base and discover that not only has Abner been there, but David has sent him away unscathed! Joab is angry and complains in no uncertain terms to David. He suggests that Abner has visited to deceive David and also to gain intelligence. Unbeknown to David, Joab then sends messengers after Abner, and on his return, under the guise of having a private conversation takes him to a secluded room and fatally stabs him. Later in the biblical record, as can be seen from the above biblical extract, we learn that the killing was a joint enterprise between Joab and Abishai.

There can be no doubt that Joab and Abishai are guilty of premeditated cold-blooded murder. The motive was clearly revenge. They wanted to be avenged for the death of their brother Asahel, who had met his death at the hands of Abner. Their thirst for retribution was not quenched by the prospect of peace in the divided kingdom, with their leader monarch of the entire nation.

They had ignored the sixth commandment which prohibits murder (their act of killing was not in the context of war). They, in effect, had rebelled against the wishes of David, their commander. Potentially they risked the rapprochement between the northern and southern kingdoms.

It should not be forgotten that this is not the only incident recorded where Joab exemplifies his capacity for merciless behaviour. He also later kills Amasa (2 Samuel 20:9-10), who David has made his army commander, probably out of envy and anger at being replaced as senior officer. Barber[71] comments:

---

[71] Cyril J. Barber, *The Books of Samuel*, Vol.2 (Neptune: Loizeaux, 2000), p.305.

> Joab, Amasa's cousin, steps forward to meet him. But his intentions are far from cordial. With cunning reminiscent of his assassination of Abner (3:27-30) he comes up to Amasa as if to kiss him. "[Is it] well [with] you, my brother?" (20:9)

It is immediately after this that Joab plunges his dagger into Amasa's belly. The wound is fatal.

Although our own thoughts for revenge may be lesser in their goals than that of Joab, any thoughts in respect of retribution must be tempered by recourse to the words of Scripture. This element is addressed in the discussion section which follows.

Discussion

First, we should examine what Scripture has to say on this important topic. Deuteronomy 32:35 states:

> It is mine to avenge; I will repay. In due time their foot will slip; the day of disaster is near and their doom rushes upon them.

The concept of God as an avenger is referred to on multiple occasions in the Old Testament (Psalms 94:1; Isaiah 1:24; 59:18; Nahum 1:2), and the Deuteronomy reference is quoted in the New Testament by Paul (Romans 12:19), and by the author of Hebrews (Hebrews 10:30). Space does not permit a fuller examination of these important texts, but Schreiner[72] provides a concise and helpful summary of the Romans text which conveys the important principle being enunciated here:

> The reference to God's wrath and leaving room for it is exceedingly important in interpreting this text. When we believers are mistreated, abused, and our rights are infringed upon, the desire for retaliation burns within us because we have been treated unjustly. We are not to give in, however, to the desire to get even. Rather, we

[72] Thomas R. Schreiner, *Romans*, BECNT (Grand Rapids: Baker Academic. 1998), p.673.

> are to place the fate of our enemies firmly in God's hands, realizing that he will repay any injustice on the last day.

Schreiner's comment is both succinct and clear. God, not us, is the instrument of retribution. This is a point to which we will return later.

When we consider Lamech, we are immediately struck by his grandiose, self-glorifying, dominant personality features. He thinks he is the man of the moment. Everything else should be subservient to his will. How dare this youth have the arrogance to confront him! He has no doubt that the youth deserved everything he got!

Judah is blind to his own double standards. It is okay for him to use the services of a prostitute, but his widowed daughter-in-law becoming pregnant outside of the sanctity of marriage? What a slut! Burn her alive! He wants revenge on her for the same sin he committed, and not only that, but in the same incident! Nevertheless, to his credit Judah confessed his sin, and as a mark of his repentance, it is recorded that he did not subsequently have sexual relations with her.

One can fully understand Simeon and Levi's motive for exacting revenge. Their (full) sister has been violated, and this by someone outside of the Israelite family. Nevertheless, their retribution was wholly out of proportion. They did not restrict their retribution to the offender, or even his immediate family, but instead went on a killing spree that included the whole settlement and its livestock.

Again, in the case of Moses, his motive is obvious. An Egyptian was beating an Israelite man, and he intervened. We cannot be certain that he intended the man's death, but that was what happened.

Gideon killed the two kings who were his prisoners of war. In those days that would arguably have been unremarkable, but his actions can be understood primarily by view of the fact that they had previously killed his brothers.

Abimelek had reasons for his multiple murders of Gideon's sons. His personality was doubtless a major factor in his mercilessness.

Doubtless his experiences during his upbringing had been a very significant factor in the moulding of his personality features.

Samson also had very understandable reasons for his actions. His is an especially complex personality with some arguably contradictory features. Although his sin is undeniable, he was greatly used by God, and, as already noted, at the end, his faith in his God is confirmed by his words.

Doeg presents as the villain of the piece with no redeeming features. He wants to ingratiate himself with King Saul, has no hesitation in informing on David to him, and no hesitation in killing a large number of men, women, and children. The king's men refused to kill God's priests. Doeg has no such compunctions. We might regard him today as a thoroughly bad lot. As a forensic psychiatrist, I would probably describe his personality in more technical terms, but the general meaning would be little different.

Joab bore a grudge – and it is easy to see why. Abner had killed his brother. Nonetheless, it is apparent from the biblical account that he did not wish to do so. Joab refused to take this into account and killed him in a planned and arguably underhand way.

A wide range of personality traits. A wide range of motives. Nevertheless, at least in most of these cases we see a propensity to take revenge for personal reasons. Generally speaking, we see God's words on vengeance in Deuteronomy being ignored. We can also see the consequences in Scripture.

The underlying message here should not be disregarded.

Chapter Nine
MARTYRDOM

Introduction

I am of Scottish origin and grew up in a Christian family. I remember from a very young age that we had a book about the Scottish Covenanters, and although I probably read but little of it, I was struck by the illustrations, for example, of a young woman bound to a stake in the sea (probably the Solway Firth), and about to be drowned when the tide rose. Aged around ten years old I heard about Jim Elliot and his martyrdom in Ecuador and was subsequently given a book describing the circumstances of this tragic event.

The name 'Covenanters' comes from the word 'covenant' which is a solemn agreement, bond by an oath, between two or more parties. Briefly, the Covenanters were those people in Scotland who signed the National Covenant in 1638. This was done to signify opposition to the interference of the Stuart kings in the concerns of the Presbyterian church of Scotland (which itself was formed by John Knox and others, and thus was Calvinist in its doctrinal approach). The Stuart kings believed in the Divine Right of Kings, but more pertinently, that they were the spiritual heads of the Church of Scotland. This latter assertion could not be accepted by the Calvinist Scots who (quite rightly) held that only the Lord Jesus Christ could be the head of a Christian church. The Covenanters were made subject to brutal persecution, and this included imprisonment, transportation, torture, and execution. Some were drowned in the Solway Firth, not far from my hometown of Dumfries.

Operation Auca was an attempt by five American missionaries to evangelise the Auca tribe of the rain forest of Ecuador. This was an isolated group of people who were known for their aggression. After several months of exchanging gifts, five male missionaries established a camp at some little distance from the Aucan settlements. They were attacked and killed. Jim Elliot, Nate Saint, Ed McCully, Peter Fleming, and Roger Youderian all died. The news was reported world-wide and occasioned an article in *Life* magazine. It should be noted that good did come out of this tragic event. The news was a catalyst to missionary efforts in the USA, and funding for missionary endeavour was substantially enhanced throughout the world. Some years later Elisabeth Elliot, the widow of Jim Elliot, and the sister of Nate Saint returned to Ecuador as missionaries. Many conversions ensued, including that of some involved in the initial missionary deaths.

History is replete with stories of martyrdom; some episodes being better remembered than others. Many will know of the title of the book, 'Foxes Book of Martyrs', although one suspects far fewer have ever read it. It begins with an account of the Emperor Nero's persecution of the Christians in first century Rome and documents the persecution of Christians in various countries in the world up until the nineteenth century. It is well worth reading, as are a plethora of other publications on the same subject.

Most Christians will be aware of the persecution of Christians in first century Rome under Nero, but unaware of other persecutory behaviour in Roman times. Although there were several periods of persecution during this period, much more widespread and severe persecution commenced in AD 303 involving a series of edicts issued by the emperors Diocletian, Maximian, Galerius, and Constantius, which removed the legal rights of Christians and demanded compliance with established Roman practice (that is, the worship of the gods of the Roman pantheon). It should be noted that Constantius was unenthusiastic in his pursuit of persecutory measures (in sharp contrast to Diocletian and Galerius), and his son Constantine is noted for his support of the Christian church – he reinstated the Christians' legal equality and restored property confiscated during persecution. Among Christians he is probably best remembered for the Council of Nicea in AD 325 when a definitive and authoritative statement was issued, the view of Arius that the Son was a created being was refuted, and the Son declared as a truly divine being, a "true God",

not created out of nothing, but begotten out of the very essence of the Father'.[73]
Although in this section of the book all the instances are taken from the New Testament, we should not forget that martyrdom is not limited to the period of the New Covenant. God's people also died for their faith under the Old Covenant, as Jesus pointed out to the scribes and the Pharisees in Matthew 23:29-31:

> 'Woe to you, teachers of the law and Pharisees, you hypocrites! You build tombs for the prophets and decorate the graves of the righteous. And you say, "If we had lived in the days of our ancestors, we would not have taken part with them in shedding the blood of the prophets." So you testify against yourselves that you are the descendants of those who murdered the prophets.'

In this section of the book, we are examining the cases of the three martyrs documented in the pages of the New Testament, specifically Stephen, James, and Antipas, and those martyred as the result of Saul's ravages on the early church. The first is extensively covered in the biblical record, that of James less so, and that of Antipas attracts but a brief mention. We should not assume that by comparison the deaths of James and Antipas are less important than that of Stephen. Nevertheless, Stephen's death was the first reported of its kind, and such a milestone event is always considered noteworthy. Despite his death and the subsequent persecution in Jerusalem, this, rather than stifling the growth of the church, paradoxically resulted in its far greater dissemination and a consequent growth in converts, both outside the confines of Jerusalem, and in other countries. Philip evangelises Samaria, is instrumental in the conversion of a senior Ethiopian official, and takes the good news of the gospel to coastal towns on the Mediterranean (Acts 8:4-40).

Acts 9:32-43 documents Peter's ministry in Lydda and in Joppa. In the following chapter we read of him preaching the gospel to a God-fearing centurion and his family with gratifying results. The aftermath of Stephen's martyrdom is the movement from Jerusalem

---

[73] Nick Needham, *2000 Years of Christ's Power,* Vol. 1 (Fearn: Christian Focus, 2016). P.223.

of persecuted Christian converts, with the spread of the gospel to Judean towns, but also to the region of Samaria, so hated by Jews in general, and also to Gentiles, such as the centurion and his household. We might like, at this stage, to remind ourselves that closer to our own time, it was under the persecution of Chairman Mao that the church in China underwent such exponential growth.
The execution of James is noteworthy because this is the death of the first Apostle. Not only that, but together with his brother John, and his fellow Apostle Peter, they comprised Jesus' inner circle, and accompanied Jesus at the time of his transfiguration, and again into the Garden of Gethsemane prior to his arrest (Mark 14:32). His arrest and subsequent death was part of a larger programme of persecution inaugurated by King Herod Agrippa I, and also included the arrest of Peter, who escaped from prison by divine intervention as recorded in Acts 12:6-19. This particular Herod (and the history of the Herodians is complicated), was one of Herod the Great's grandsons. (Herod the Great was the individual who was responsible for killing the infants in Bethlehem around the time of Jesus' birth as recorded in Matthew 2:16-18).

Agrippa I was strongly influenced by Rome and its culture. Indeed, this is hardly surprising as after his father's execution in 7 BC he was brought up in Rome, in close proximity to imperial power. Following the accession of Claudius, the territory he ruled was almost as extensive as that governed by his grandfather, but his reign ended abruptly with his death (Acts 12:20-23). Herod had to answer directly to Caesar in Rome, his territory was a known region of unrest within the Roman Empire, and hence his clamping down on the nascent Christian church. He didn't want anything to threaten the peace and was doubtless aware that removing the leadership might cripple the movement.

The personage of Antipas[74] comes years after the deaths of Stephen and James. How much later is a matter for conjecture and to some extent depends on the date of writing of the Book of Revelation. Here is not the place to rehearse the arguments for and against a late or early date for this particular book. Nevertheless, it is clear from this (and indeed from the letters to the other six churches) that the gospel had spread extensively from its early days in Jerusalem). Although

---

[74] Revelation 2:13.

virtually nothing is recorded about Antipas' death, we do have information about Pergamum itself. It was a large and important city. There was a strong concentration on idolatry there with temples to a number of gods, including Zeus, Athene, Dionysos, and Asklepios. The latter is of some interest to me as a doctor as Asklepios was the god of healing. Emperor worship was also a major feature of the ethos in Pergamum (as it was in other cities of the seven in Asia mentioned in the book of Revelation). Nevertheless, Pergamum was the centre of this imperial cult, and it has been suggested that this may be the basis for the statement in Revelation 2:12: 'where Satan has his throne'. Although Christians in Pergamum are commended for their devotion, it is clear from the account in Revelation 2:12-17 that all was not as it should have been in the church there. Some were engaging in pagan worship and in sexual immorality. Yet there was still clear authentic witness to the gospel message, as evidenced by the killing of Antipas.

Paul is the odd man out here. He was not only a victim of persecution, but also a perpetrator.

Having briefly considered the relevant background, we will now proceed to examine the deaths in more detail.

STEPHEN

Acts 7:51-58

> 'You stiff-necked people! Your hearts and ears are still uncircumcised. You are just like your ancestors: you always resist the Holy Spirit! Was there ever a prophet your ancestors did not persecute? They even killed those who predicted the coming of the Righteous One. And now you have betrayed and murdered him – you who have received the law that was given through angels but have not obeyed it.'
>
> When the members of the Sanhedrin heard this, they were furious and gnashed their teeth at him. But Stephen, full of the Holy Spirit, looked up to heaven and saw the glory of God, and Jesus standing at the right

> hand of God. 'Look,' he said, 'I see heaven open and the Son of Man standing at the right hand of God.'
>
> At this they covered their ears and, yelling at the top of their voices, they all rushed at him, dragged him out of the city and began to stone him. Meanwhile, the witnesses laid their coats at the feet of a young man named Saul.

The brief excerpt from Scripture above furnishes the outcome of the trial or lynching of the Christian martyr Stephen. The story seems to include elements of both, and they are intertwined in Luke's account.

The rather lengthy account begins in Acts 6:8 with Stephen's arrest. Although Acts 6:1-6 outlines his service in serving tables as a result of the Hellenists' claim that their widows were being 'overlooked in the daily distribution of food' (Acts 6:1), it is clear that his gifts did not stop there, for he was also able to perform 'great wonders and signs among the people' (Acts 6:8). He would thus have likely been well known to the general populace as an impressive proponent of the nascent Christian movement. His oration, reproduced in Acts 7:2 to 7:53 indicates that he was also gifted as a powerful preacher. This, incidentally, is the longest speech in the Book of Acts.

The hostility against Stephen is initiated by those who belonged to the 'Synagogue of the Freedmen' (Acts 6:9). This refers to Jews who at one point had been slaves but subsequently been freed. Among them may well have been descendants of Jews who were enslaved during Pompey's invasion of Palestine in 63 BC, taken to Rome, and then they, or at least some of them, when freed, returned to their roots in Jerusalem. Stephen is seized and taken before the Sanhedrin for trial. His opponents falsely accuse him of speaking against the temple and the law. This is ironic in itself as by bringing fabricated evidence they themselves are guilty of breaking the law, specifically the ninth commandment: 'You shall not give false testimony against your neighbour' (Exodus 20:16).

Stephen is asked by the high priest whether the charges he faces are true. As Peterson[75] avers, 'Stephen develops a scriptural argument which charges Israel with consistently rejecting God and those sent to fulfil his purpose for his people (Acts 7:9-10, 23-29, 33-43)'. Although space does not permit a detailed examination of his discourse, it ends with the death of Jesus, and the barbed accusation that 'you who have received the law that was given through angels but have not obeyed it' (Acts 7:53).

Accusing the self-satisfied interpreters of the law of breaking it! (He had also levelled the same charge against their ancestors). They were, at the very least, not well disposed towards Stephen from the start. Such accusations were perceived as an affront, and 'they were furious and gnashed their teeth at him' (Acts 7:54). They were incandescent with rage. The outcome of this encounter could not be in doubt.

Stephen then has a vision of heaven which he communicates to those present: '"Look," he said, "I see heaven open and the Son of Man standing at the right hand of God"' (Acts 7:56). This was too much for the members of the Sanhedrin. They covered their ears in an attempt to ignore words they regarded as blasphemy, dragged him out of the city, and stoned him.

Interestingly here, and almost as a footnote, we find the statement, 'Meanwhile the witnesses laid their coats at the feet of a young man named Saul' (Acts 7:58). Hardly the most auspicious entry into New Testament history for the man who was to be so pivotal in the future spread of Christianity.

Stephen is accused of blasphemy, and in such circumstances it was appropriate for his case to be heard before the council of the Jews, the Sanhedrin. The accusations were fabricated which in itself was a breach of Mosaic law as already noted. Those present are infuriated at Stephen's (correct) accusations and after his account of his vision, the crowd rises up (probably also including at least some of the members of the Sanhedrin), drags him out of the city, and stones him

---

[75] David G. Peterson, *The Acts of the Apostles*, Pillar (Grand Rapids: Eerdmans, 2009), p.244.

to death. As Vickers[76] notes, there is debate as to whether this constitutes an official stoning or is the consequence of mob violence. He avers 'it is both – even if the council does not direct the action, Stephen is standing before them, and it is impossible to think that the mob is doing anything the council wishes to stop'. He also thinks it likely that some Sanhedrin members constitute part of the mob. This is most definitely illegal. Not only has there not been a recognised hearing before the Sanhedrin, but also the country is under Roman control, and only they can authorise the death penalty, the Sanhedrin cannot. Old Testament law might prescribe execution, but the governing authority is the only one which can sanction it. Irrespective of this, a lynch mob enacts its own justice.

SAUL

Acts 8:1-3

> And Saul approved of their killing him.
>
> On that day a great persecution broke out against the church in Jerusalem, and all except the apostles were scattered throughout Judea and Samaria. Godly men buried Stephen and mourned deeply for him. But Saul began to destroy the church. Going from house to house, he dragged off both men and women and put them in prison.

Readers should be aware from the start that the Saul referred to here is not King Saul of the Old Testament but the Apostle Paul, who is referred to by this name in the Bible prior to his missionary journey to Cyprus, and thereafter as Paul (Acts 13:9).

The Scripture reproduced above follows immediately on from the martyrdom of Stephen, discussed in the previous chapter. Saul was a devout Jew. Indeed, he was later to testify before King Agrippa during his detention in Caesarea under Porcius Festus, that in time past he 'conformed to the strictest sect of our religion, living as a Pharisee' (Acts 26:5). Paul acted on the basis of his convictions of

---

76 Brian J. Vickers, *John-Acts*, Expository Commentary (Wheaton: Crossway, p.405.

that point in time, that is, his erroneous beliefs, concerning the Christian faith.

Following the death of Stephen of which, as the Scripture quoted above informs us, he approved, he became active in the persecution which followed. The Greek word translated 'destroy' in the NIV (Acts 8:3), is a particularly strong word, and arguably better rendered as 'ravaging' as it is in the ESV, NASB, and CSB. So far as judicial sentencing is concerned, Schnabel[77] suggests this would probably have ranged from flogging (the forty lashes minus one), to the death sentence.

It will doubtless have been noted by some readers that the passage quoted above does not explicitly state that those, or some of those persecuted by Saul in Jerusalem were indeed killed, but that this was the case is confirmed by Luke in Acts 22:4 where he quotes Paul as saying, 'I persecuted the followers of this Way to their death'. Again, in Acts 26:10 Paul is quoted as saying, 'on the authority of the chief priests I put many of the Lord's people in prison, and when they were put to death, I cast my vote against them'. Truly, there was blood on Saul's hands.

When we think of Paul today, we usually think of him in his post-conversion days. We remember his missionary journeys, his letters which comprise so much of our New Testament, and the Christian tradition of his death in Rome. Our minds tend to shy away from recalling his persecution of the nascent church. Paul's mind did not, as can be readily seen from his later writings. In Acts 22:19-20, after his arrest in Jerusalem (which followed his third missionary journey), the Roman commander of the arresting soldiers allowed him to address the assembled mob. Paul there attested that he went from synagogue to synagogue to imprison and beat Christian believers. In Galatians 1:13, he refers to 'how intensely I persecuted the church of God and tried to destroy it'. Indeed, it is apt here to recall his words to Timothy in 1 Timothy 1:15, where, when considering the subject of sinners, he avers, 'I am the worst'. MacArthur[78] comments here:

---

[77] Eckhard J. Schnabel, *Acts*, ZECNT (Grand Rapids: Zondervan, 2012), p.395.
[78] John MacArthur, *1 Timothy* (Chicago: Moody, 1995), p.33.

> Many in our day would hasten to correct Paul's self-image and restore his self-esteem. But that was a healthy self-view for Paul because it was accurate. It's hard to imagine anyone worse than a blasphemer of God and persecutor of His church. Such a view of himself also served to keep Paul humble and grateful.

Paul was acutely aware of his past sin. He knew it was forgiven by God but he himself did not forget it. As MacArthur states, he was 'humble and grateful'. So also should we be.

JAMES

Acts 12:1-2

> It was about this time that King Herod arrested some who belonged to the church, intending to persecute them. He had James, the brother of John, put to death with the sword. When he saw that this met with approval among the Jews, he proceeded to seize Peter also.

The family history of the Herodians is not wholly straightforward, and care is needed to identify what position individual Herods occupy in the family tree. As has already been noted, the Herod referred to here is Herod Agrippa I (c. 9 BC-AD 44), the grandson of Herod the Great). He was quite popular with the Jewish leadership, despite being brought up and educated in Rome. Indeed, during that time he was friends with both Gaius (Caligula), and Claudius, both future Roman emperors. One notes in passing that Herod's lifestyle in Rome was far from irreproachable and he was regarded as being something of a waster. Indeed, at one point he had to leave Rome because of his indebtedness.

It is worth recalling here that in terms of the foreign territories ruled by Rome, those territories which were settled and peaceful came under the authority of the Roman senate - it appointed those who were to govern over them. Potential trouble-spots (and Judea certainly fitted into this category), had rulers directly appointed by the emperor. Herod would have had to answer to Caesar for untoward events in his area of jurisdiction. This, undoubtedly, would have been at the forefront of his mind and influenced his decision making. It is also worth remembering in this context that the same applied to Pilate, and he would have been well aware of it when dealing with the case of Jesus. Herod thus had a strong vested interest in the maintenance of peace in his land. He wanted to appease the Jewish leaders, and hence the execution of James.

James was one of the Apostles and thus a prominent leader of the Christian movement. It has long been a strategy of regimes to quell dissidence in their countries by removing the opposition leaders (although this paradoxically often results in the opposite effect). Encouraged by the favourable response of the Jews to this act, Herod arrests Peter, although his likely violent intentions towards him were thwarted by Peter's miraculous escape from prison (Acts 12:6-10).

James was put to death by the sword. Whether this means he was run through or beheaded is uncertain. Bock[79] thinks he was probably beheaded, although given Jewish attitudes to this method of execution, he does not exclude the possibility of him being run through.

James is thus the second recorded person to die as a martyr after Stephen (Acts 7:54-60). It is, nonetheless, significant to note that he is the first Apostle to die for his faith. All because Herod wanted to please the Jews and avoid being seen in a bad light by Rome.

So far as the legal justification for the execution of James is concerned, it is possible that Agrippa found James to be apostate so far as the Jewish faith is concerned (although the legal grounds for this are questionable at best). With respect to his authority for doing so is concerned, he was the Roman client king.[80] His political situation has already been outlined, and thus the motivation underpinning the execution of James (and potentially Peter) is clear.

Once again, as with the death of Stephen, instead of stifling the nascent Christian church, James' death had the opposite effect from that intended. Although it pleased the Jews, as has happened

---

[79] Darrell L. Bock, *Acts*, BECNT (Grand Rapids: Baker Academic, 2007), p.425.
[80] Craig S. Keener, *Acts*, Vol.2 (Grand Rapids: Baker Academic, p.1873-1874.

repeatedly in history from New Testament times on, persecution strengthened the church and stimulated growth.

ANTIPAS

Revelation 2:12-17

> 'To the angel of the church in Pergamum write:
>
> > These are the words of him who has the sharp, double-edged sword. I know where you live – where Satan has his throne. Yet you remain true to my name. You did not renounce your faith in me, not even in the days of Antipas, my faithful witness, who was put to death in your city – where Satan lives.
> >
> > Nevertheless, I have a few things against you: there are some among you who hold to the teaching of Baalam, who taught Balak to entice the Israelites to sin so that they ate food sacrificed to idols and committed sexual immorality. Likewise, you also have those who hold to the teaching of the Nicolaitans. Repent therefore! Otherwise, I will soon come to you and will fight against them with the sword of my mouth.
> >
> > Whoever has ears, let them hear what the Spirit says to the churches. To the one who is victorious, I will give some of the hidden manna. I will also give that person a white stone with a new name written on it, known only to the one who receives it.

This passage comes from the well-known letters to the seven churches of Asia (what we now know as modern Turkey, but the Romans referred to this expanse of land as Asia). Our primary concern here is, of course, Antipas, but it is appropriate to place it in some degree of context.

The Book of Revelation is addressed to seven churches, and each church receives comments on their distinguishing features, both good and bad. As Phillips[81] comments, it should be noted that these communications were not sent separately to each individual church, but were sent as one complete whole to be read by all the churches. It is arguably the case that they do have contemporary relevance in that they can also be viewed as directed at all churches throughout the gospel age. We should not neglect the points made, but rather, should make reference to them in the appraisal of our own church and churches today.

The church in question here is that of Pergamum. It was a magnificent city and was probably the capital of the Roman province of Asia. As already noted, the cult of the (Roman) emperor was strong here, and there were many temples, attesting to the syncretistic nature of religion in the Greco-Roman world. The Christians (and the Jews) stood apart from this acceptance and worship of a plethora of gods, by their monotheism. Although the church at Pergamum attracted praise for its faithfulness, there was tolerance of non-Christian beliefs, and for this they are criticised. The story of Balaam (Numbers 22-24) is well known, and he fomented the Israelites to engage in false worship and sexual immorality with the Moabites. In Pergamum we might infer that what is being referred to here is some form of participation in pagan worship combined with sexual immorality.

The earlier letter to the church at Smyrna had warned of impending persecution (Revelation 2:10), and this to the point of death. It is clear that such oppression has already arrived in Pergamum with the death of Antipas, described as 'my faithful witness'.

Scripture records but little about Antipas, other than he was a faithful witness for Christ, and was put to death in Pergamum. Although we are not told as to the mode of execution, tradition has it that he was roasted to death inside a brass bull during the reign of Domitian (AD 81-96). He may have been one of the leaders of the church at Pergamum. This would certainly explain why he might have been prominent in the fellowship there and singled out for exemplary treatment. True to the words of the proclamation to the Christians of the city, he had not renounced his faith in Christ.

---

[81] Richard D. Phillips, *Revelation*, REC (Phillipsburg: P & R, 2017), p.111.

Nevertheless, despite the presence of false teaching (Revelation 2:14-15), it is recorded of the church there that, 'You remain true to my name. You did not renounce your faith in me, not even in the days of Antipas, my faithful witness, who was put to death in your city – where Satan lives' (Revelation 2:13). As MacArthur[82] comments on Antipas:

> Here was a man who paid the ultimate price for his refusal to compromise. Because of his faithfulness, the risen Lord commended Antipas with a title used elsewhere to refer to Himself (Revelation 1:5; 3:14). Antipas' faithfulness and courage were a rebuke to those at Pergamum who were tempted to compromise with the world.

Antipas can be described as a martyr for the faith. It is worth briefly considering here the origin of this word as it is of direct relevance to this passage of Scripture. The word in this passage translated as 'witness' is the Greek word *martus*. As Osborne[83] points out, this term did not take the meaning of 'martyr' as we currently understand it until the third century, but the link is made here with the association between witnessing for the faith and death as its consequence.

As no details are provided, it is impossible to make authoritative comment. Given the strong affinity of Pergamum as a city with Roman culture, one might well think that Antipas' death was the result of some formal legal action on the part of the authorities. If, as tradition suggests, Antipas' death occurred during the reign of Domitian, it is relevant to consider here that Eusebius, writing in the fourth century, refers to severe persecution of Christians towards the end of his reign. On the other hand, contemporary writers give no information of trials and executions by way of confirmation. The latter, of course, represents an argument from silence, and arguably from lack of surviving records rather than comprising actual contradiction.

---

[82] John MacArthur, *Revelation 1-11* (Chicago: Moody, 1999), p.87.
[83] Grant R. Osborne, *Revelation*, BECNT (Grand Rapids: Baker Academic, 2002), p.142-143.

Many have, are, and will follow in Antipas' footsteps. This is often forgotten or neglected in parts of the world today where our faith can be freely practiced. We should pay much more attention to the many places where Christians are severely persecuted for their beliefs.

DISCUSSION

In the West we are not generally at risk from dying for our faith. Sadly, it is often forgotten or it conveniently slips from our minds that in other parts of the world this is a very real possibility. An article from 'Christianity Today'[84] in 2021 reports that:

- Every day, 13 Christians worldwide are killed because of their faith
- Every day, 12 churches or Christian buildings are attacked
- Every day, 12 Christians are unjustly arrested or imprisoned, and another 5 are abducted.

Other shocking statistics, taken from the article, '10 Facts about Persecution from the 2021 World Watch List'[85] include the following:

- More Christians are murdered in Nigeria than in any other country
- North Korea has held the title of "world's worst persecutor of Christians" for 20 consecutive years
- Approximately 91 percent of recorded violent killings of Christians for faith-related reasons took place in Africa
- In Latin America, drug cartels are the largest threat to religious freedom
- The world's largest democracy, India, is among the top 10 most difficult countries to be a Christian.

---

84 https://www.christianitytoday.com/news/2021/January/christian-persecution -2021-countries -open-doors-watch-list.html (Accessed 09/03/2022).

85 https://www.frc.org/updatearticle/20210114/facts-persecution (Accessed 09/03/2022).

Just the few bald statements reproduced above provide some idea of the persecution and ever real threat of death faced by Christians in other parts of the globe. That the church is properly the congregation of all genuine Christians worldwide means that believers everywhere are part of the same family. That means that those persecuted and killed are *our* brothers and sisters in Christ. Such should give us pause for thought, and more than that, to consideration as to what we, in much more fortunate circumstances, could and should be doing to assist them in their unenviable circumstances.

We should not forget, or indeed be ignorant of, past religious persecution in the UK itself. Although it is not possible here to explore this to any great extent, we might like to remember, for example, that with the passing of Henry VIII, who split with the Pope and established the Church of England, he persecuted radical Protestants who opposed some of the changes. His successor, Edward VI supported the Reformation, and persecution of Protestants ceased, but the next to the throne was Queen Mary I, a Catholic, and she instigated persecution of the Protestants. Indeed, it was during her reign that reformers such as Thomas Cranmer, Hugh Latimer, and George Wishart were executed along with many others. Interestingly their executions resulted in many joining the church rather than having the opposite effect of acting to suppress their faith. When Elizabeth I came to the throne next, she was a Protestant, and the pendulum swung the other way, with the Catholics now being the target for persecution. Religious struggle continued in the English Civil War between 1642 and 1651, Oliver Cromwell's forces proving victorious.

The founding of the American State can be regarded as a consequence of religious persecution in England (and other parts of Europe). Many of the colonies who pioneered the settlements in North America were comprised of people who had strong religious convictions and left Europe where they were being persecuted, for a new home where they could worship God according to their own conscience. Most people have heard of the ship 'Mayflower', containing English families known as the Pilgrims who separated themselves from the Church of England, believing it beyond hope of appropriate reform, and settled in Massachusetts. Such is still the position for many today, for example, Christians leaving Iran and becoming asylum seekers in the UK and in other countries.

Turning last to the present day, the question has been asked, 'Are Christians persecuted in Britain?' At first glance this may appear a superfluous enquiry as in the UK, the USA, and many other developed countries, Christians are not being executed or imprisoned for their faith, and neither are their churches being burned down. Nevertheless, one arguably should take a nuanced approach. Andrea Williams[86], the CEO of Christian Concern and the Christian Legal Centre has commented as follows:

> Extreme persecution doesn't just come out of nowhere. It develops over time as a society's attitudes towards Christianity change. There is a scale of persecution where at one end there are more serious forms (execution, imprisonment, torture) and at the other there are less serious forms (exclusion, marginalisation, discrimination). I think it's hard to deny that in Britain we're on this latter end of the scale.

This is a perceptive statement and worthy of careful consideration. One significant observation is the concept of a gradual slide into persecutory attitudes in society. Certainly there are strong hints, indeed concrete evidence that such is happening today in the UK Much, of course, depends on the interpretation of the word 'persecution'. The Shorter Oxford English Dictionary[87] defines this as being, 'The action of persecuting, *esp.* the infliction of death, torture, or penalties for adherence to a particular religious belief or opinion'. There is clearly scope for nuances of interpretation here, particularly in terms of the last phrase.

No one will seriously argue that imprisonment, torture and execution are faced by Christians in the UK today, but there are a number of troubling cases reported by Wyatt in an article entitled, 'Investigation: Are Christians in the UK persecuted?'[88]:

---

[86] https://www.reform-magazine.co.uk/2013/10/a-good-question-are-christians -persecuted-in-britain/ (Accessed 10/03/2022).

[87] *The Shorter Oxford English Dictionary*, Vol II (London: Guild, 1983), p.1559.

[88] https://www.premierchristianity.com/features/investigation-are-christians-in-the-uk-persecuted-/4366.article (Accessed 10/03/2022).

- Lillian Ladele, a registrar for the London Borough of Islington, who was disciplined for refusing to officiate at civil partnerships when they were legalised in 2005 took the council to court claiming discrimination on the grounds of her religious beliefs. The Court of Appeal and the European Court of Human Rights concluded that Islington had acted fairly.
- In 2020, Dominic Muir preached as he had done hundreds of times before in a Somerset town centre. He was forced to stop by a police officer. A subsequent letter to the chief constable threatening to sue the force produced a financial settlement.

There have been many cases of street preachers being arrested, of nurses disciplined for praying with their patient, of workers being forced to cover up their cross necklaces, and council workers dismissed for their refusal to conduct services of marriage for same sex couples. Whether or not one regards these as persecution or not, they provide strong evidence to support Andrea Williams' assertion that we are on a slippery slope.

The current liberal attitudes being promulgated by prominent figures (often described by the term 'woke'), in terms of sexuality are wholly contrary to the teachings of Scripture and should be recognised for what they are. Pointing this out will inevitably bring Christians into more conflict with the authorities.

The outlook cannot be regarded as rosy, but neither was it promised so. Jesus said this in Luke 21:16:

> You will be betrayed even by parents, brothers and sisters, relatives and friends, and they will put some of you to death.

We will leave the last word in this section to Desiderius Erasmus:[89]

[89] Esther Chung-Kim and Todd R. Hains, eds., A*cts*, Reformation *Commentary on Scripture*, New Testament VI (Downers Grove: IVP Academic, 2014), p.105.

Among Christians the death of those who perish for the sake of the glory of Christ is worthy of applause and triumphal celebration. If there are some tears there, they are not shed for the one who has died, but either for the murderers who invoke hell upon themselves, or for the flock deprived of its needed shepherd.

Chapter Ten
FINAL COMMENTS

This book has covered a broad swathe of intentionally caused loss of life over several millennia, encompassing a wide range of countries, cultures, motives, and modes of inflicting death. Many of the incidents included will likely have engendered diversion of the reader's thought into other, albeit connected areas. In a volume of this size only relatively superficial coverage of the material is possible, and with this in mind, concluding remarks are confined to three areas.

One theme that kept recurring in my mind as I wrote was the attributes of God, and in particular the holiness of God. A second matter which I felt to be important was the application of any lessons to the lives of Christians today. A third was what is often referred to in common parlance as 'the elephant in the room'. This is undoubtedly a poor description of what it refers to, as it is wholly unsuitable in terms of appropriate reverence, albeit readily understandable in its import.

The attributes of God

Pink,[90] in the preface to his book 'The Attributes of God' states 'The foundation of all true knowledge of God must be a clear mental apprehension of His perfections as revealed in Holy Scripture'. ('Perfections' is another term for attributes, and in some ways is preferable in that it implies the flawless quality of those characteristics we ascribe to the divine being).

[90] Arthur W. Pink, *The Attributes of God* (Grand Rapids: Baker, 1975), p.7.

Central to the character of God is his holiness. It is unfortunate indeed that appreciation of this vitally important subject is so lacking in Christians today. This deficit cannot be attributed to lack of available literature on this topic. One might think here particularly of R. C. Sproul's[91] book on the subject which has attracted much favourable comment and has sold in excess of a quarter of a million copies. In the book Sproul himself volunteers his own difficulties early in his Christian life with the same type of issues which have been discussed in these pages, and continue to occupy Christians today:[92]

> My "conversion" to God the Father was not without its attending difficulties. Though I was deeply impressed by the notion of a God who created a whole universe from nothing, I was troubled by the fact that the world we live in is a place filled with sorrows. It is a world riddled with evil. My next question was, How could a good and holy God create a world that is in such a mess? As I studied the Old Testament, I was also bothered by the stories about God's ordering the slaughter of women and children, of God's killing Uzzah instantly for touching the ark of the covenant, and by other narratives that seemed to reveal a brutal side to the character of God. How could I ever come to love such a God?
>
> The one concept, the central idea I kept meeting in Scripture, was the idea that God is *holy*. The word was foreign to me. I wasn't sure what it meant. I made the question a matter of diligent and persistent search. Today I am still absorbed with the question of the holiness of God. I am convinced that it is one of the most important ideas that a Christian can ever grapple with. It is basic to our whole understanding of God and of Christianity.

Arguably a major cause of a general lack of appreciation of the holiness of God (and his attributes generally) is the insufficient

[91] R.C. Sproul, *The Holiness of God* (Carol Stream: Tyndale, 1998),
[92] Ibid, p.11.

attention afforded to it from the pulpit, and in other areas of church life.

In modern church life it is common to hear the phrases ‘God is love’ and ‘God loves you’, or similar, repeated over and over again. Here, I am in no way trying to disparage this message, indeed, quite the reverse. What is open to criticism is the way in which this one attribute of God is promulgated at the expense of the other attributes. To present God simply in a one-dimensional manner is potentially to misrepresent the fullness of God’s character. This is open to disastrous conclusions. A sinner whose sole impression of God is that his character can simply be encompassed by the word ‘love’ might arguably reasonably assume that a loving God would not consign them to eternal condemnation. It is not difficult to appreciate the potential for the misrepresentation of the gospel message. Here, this one-dimensional impression of God has not been balanced by other aspects of his character, such as his justice.

Nevertheless, despite emphasising God’s holiness, there is valid argument that his holiness and his love belong together. In Hosea 11:8-9 we read:

> ‘How can I give you up, Ephraim? How can I hand you over, Israel? How can I make you like Admah? How can I make you lie Zeboyim? My heart is changed within me; all my compassion is aroused. I will not carry out my fierce anger, nor will I devastate Ephraim again. For I am God, and not a man – the Holy One among you.’

Hosea speaks here of God as ‘the Holy One’, completely different from human beings, and this includes in his love. He doesn’t give up Israel, despite its unfaithfulness. Human beings would have given up someone like Hosea’s wife, but God doesn’t; even in his love he is totally different from us.

God’s holiness also means that he opposes those who trample on the poor, the widow, the orphan and the foreigner. So God’s holiness and deep sense of what is pure and good is something to rejoice about. We should also rejoice that although God’s holiness means he does not and can not tolerate sin, in Jesus Christ he sees us as perfect. Our sins were imputed to him at Calvary, and his righteousness has been imputed to us. Rejoice indeed!

A proper understanding of God's attributes is not merely the province of the pastor. If the congregation is to be active in the propagation of the gospel message (and some appear to think this is the sole responsibility of the pulpit), they too must have an appreciation of the subject, although arguably the impetus should be pulpit-driven.
It is hoped that in the preceding pages the holiness of God has been apparent. In the study guide accompanying his teaching series on 'The Attributes of God', Lawson[93] writes:

> To many people today, holiness is a foreign concept. For the authors of Scripture, however, holiness is one of God's most prominent attributes. It denotes both His separation from creation as the infinitely superior One and His absolute moral purity.

On the following page, Lawson makes the following observations on God's moral perfection:

1. God is completely without sin or moral blemish.
2. All of God's decisions and judgements are perfect.
3. As an infinitely holy being, God is not neutral toward good or evil.
    a. God takes delight in all that is true, worthy, and upright.
    b. Because God's very nature is one of purity, He cannot tolerate sin.
    c. It is only through the righteousness of Jesus Christ that guilty sinners can be reconciled to God.

Beeke and Smalley[94] comment that, 'The general decline of godly fear among professing Christians today is directly related to an

---

[93] Steven J. Lawson, *The Attributes of God* (Sanford: Ligonier Ministries. 2013), p.19.
[94] Joel R. Beeke and Paul M. Smalley, *Revelation and God, Vol.1, Reformed Systematic Theology* (Wheaton: Crossway, 2019), p.581.

ignorance of God's holiness'. This is a remarkably perceptive statement.

When we are more attuned to the holiness of God, we no longer cringe at the mass destruction of the flood, or the killing of Canaanites. Rather, we may marvel at the patience (another of God's attributes), of God. He had put up with the sin of the original inhabitants of the earth for an indeterminate length of time (1 Peter 3:20), and that of the Canaanites for hundreds of years. We should not wonder at how God could destroy nations when he did – rather we should marvel that he did not do so long before. We should likewise marvel at his tolerance with us before saving us from the consequences of our sin through the perfect sacrifice of his Son, Jesus. God continues to show patience in our age (2 Peter 3:15).

The power over life and death is with God. This is subsumed to man in the case of the prescribed death penalty for acts of murder. It is easy to appreciate why God forbids murder – we don't like murder either. It is sin and is forbidden in the sixth commandment. But God's commands are properly understood in the context of his character, and this inevitably leads us to back to the holiness of God.

Having a greater appreciation of the character of God is an essential prerequisite for Christian living in general, but is of great importance in worship, teaching, and every other aspect of the personal and corporate Christian journey.

The Christian life today

Christians would shrink from any suggestion that they would be capable of murder. Yet, although the sermon on the mount is well recognised as an entity, its contents and their implications are less well internalised. Matthew 5:21-26, part of this discourse, reads as follows:

> 'You have heard that it was said to the people long ago, "You shall not murder, and anyone who murders will be subject to judgement." But I tell you that anyone who is angry with a brother or sister will be subject to judgement. Again, anyone who says to a brother or sister, "Raca," is answerable to the court. And anyone

> who says, "You fool!" will be in danger of the fire of hell. Therefore, if you are offering your gift at the altar and there remember that your brother or sister has something against you, leave your gift there in front of the altar. First go and be reconciled to them; then come and offer your gift. Settle matters quickly with your adversary who is taking you to court. Do it while you are still together on the way, or your adversary may hand you over to the officer, and you may be thrown into prison. Truly I tell you, you will not get out until you have paid the last penny.'

Jesus here quotes from the sixth of the ten commandments (Exodus 20:13; Deuteronomy 5:17). Its effect was, as MacArthur[95] notes, 'to shatter the illusion of self-righteousness'. The scribes and Pharisees could congratulate themselves that whatever else they might have done, they had not committed murder. As is seen in so many other instances in the Gospels, they were (and wanted to be seen as) meticulous in scrupulous adherence to the letter of the law (Torah). The implications of what flowed from that law were ignored. Jesus was not merely concerned just with obedience to the letter of the law and no more. He was expounding a deeper understanding of the implications of the divine instructions.

Although it is not proposed to discuss this passage in detail here, the general principles are clear. Jesus is pointing out that the forbidden act of murder does not in itself arise from empty space – it has antecedents in the emotions. Most of the time, these thoughts will not culminate in the completed act of murder, but the sinful thoughts themselves are potential antecedents. Contemplation of such concepts should have been sufficient to dispel the self-righteousness of the scribes and Pharisees (and in us also).

Righteous anger is not being prohibited here. We might infer that righteous anger was what Jesus exhibited in his cleansing of the temple in John 2:13-17, when he found his Father's house being dishonoured by commerce. We might also recall that Jesus is described as angry in Mark 3:5 when he went into the synagogue and was being closely observed by those 'looking for a reason to accuse

---

[95] John MacArthur, *Matthew 1-7* (Chicago: Moody, 1983), p.291.

Jesus' to see whether he would heal the man with the shrivelled hand on the Sabbath. Edwards[96] describes Jesus' anger here as 'a description of righteous indignation'.

Essentially here, Jesus is pointing to the emotions arising from the heart (or our innermost being), which are connected with, and precede, sinful actions. As an analogy from medical concepts, physical actions are preceded by cerebral cogitation (thought) which results in messages being transmitted through the nervous system to the muscles which will contract to effect the physical action desired. Sinful physical acts are predicated by sinful thoughts. Jesus is warning against not only the sinful actions, but also against the sinful thoughts which precede them. In terms of logic, such argument is simple and compelling.

Jesus goes on to make similar comments relating to other offences against his holy law, for example, in Matthew 5:27-30, in terms of the sin of adultery: 'But I tell you that anyone who looks at a woman lustfully has already committed adultery with her in his heart'.

As a doctor, I would regard such directives as being somewhat akin to the field of preventative medicine. If the precursors to catastrophe are eliminated, the otherwise inevitable disaster will not occur. Jesus is using irrefutable logic here. Nevertheless, despite accepting this, we must internalise and act on these words.

The absent event

What has been missing from this book so far is in fact glaringly obvious and is unlikely to have been missed by readers.

The most important death of the most significant individual in the whole of history is, of course, that of Jesus. Although not referred to in the body of this text, I hope its presence has been implicit throughout.

---

[96] James R. Edwards, *The Gospel According to Mark*, Pillar (Grand Rapids. Eerdmans, 2002), p.101.

The death and resurrection of the Lord Jesus Christ is central to Christianity. Grudem[97] defines the atonement as 'the work Christ did in his life and death to earn our salvation'. God could have, with perfect justice, have left us in our sin, and with the inevitable judgement. He did not, and that this is so is a consequence of his attribute of love (John. 3:16). One theological dictionary[98] describes the word 'atonement' as 'the removal or forgiveness of sin through a sacrifice, resulting in God's appeasement' (Exodus 32:30-32). By appeasement we essentially mean that the rightful wrath of God at sin has been satisfied.

The Lord Jesus Christ lived a perfect sinless life, and in his death at Calvary paid the price for our sins. His sacrifice can be seen as being anticipated by the Old Testament sacrificial system, while acting as a type (or foreshadowing of) the definitive act to come, was not a complete answer to the problem of sin, because those sacrifices were offered repeatedly, whereas, as the writer of Hebrews reminds us (referring to Jesus), 'For by one sacrifice he has made perfect for ever those who are being made holy' (Hebrews 10:14).

The resurrection of Jesus indicates that God was satisfied with his work on the cross. 1 Corinthians 15:23 describes Christ in his resurrection as the 'firstfruits'. This latter term refers to the first sheaf of the grain harvest,[99] and this means that the rest of the harvest, in other words, those who belong to Christ (that is, Christians), will also rise and be with him in glory. It is no surprise that the theme of the resurrection, with its message of certain hope, was a cardinal feature of the witness of the early church.

The death and resurrection of Christ has not overtly featured in the body of this book, but it is the central pivot of the Bible and the Christian message as a whole.

This book has featured many disturbing, indeed shocking events which tax our intellect and emotions. It is thus with joy that we can

---

[97] Wayne Grudem, *Systematic Theology* (Grand Rapids: Zondervan, 1994), p.568.

[98] Matthew S. DeMoss and J. Edward Miller, *Zondervan Dictionary of Bible and Theology Words* (Grand Rapids: Zondervan, 2002), p.31.

[99] David E. Garland, *1 Corinthians*, BECNT (Grand Rapids: Baker Academic, 2003), p.705.

end on a triumphal note with the glorious message of the gospel. In the words of Jude's doxology (Jude 24-25):

> To him who is able to keep you from stumbling and to present you before his glorious presence without fault and with great joy – to the only God our Saviour be glory, majesty, power and authority, through Jesus Christ our Lord, before all ages, now and forevermore! Amen.

Other Books By The Same Author

ISBN: 9781913181697 ISBN: 9781913181857 ISBN: 9781913181550

More information on all these insightful titles can be found at:

www.faithbuilderspublishing.co.uk/shop

9781913181925
BV - #0024 - 040823 - C0 - 229/152/11 - PB - 9781913181925 - Gloss Lamination